Library Service to Spanish Speaking Patrons

Library Service to Spanish Speaking Patrons

A Practical Guide

Sharon Chickering Moller

2001
Libraries Unlimited, Inc.
Englewood, Colorado

To Pete, who introduced me to Latin America,
and to Pilar and Felicia, who keep
me on the journey.

Libraries Unlimited, Inc.
P.O. Box 6633
Englewood, CO 80155-6633
1-800-237-6124
www.lu.com

Library of Congress Cataloging-in-Publication Data

Moller, Sharon Chickering.
  Library service to Spanish speaking patrons : a practical guide / Sharon Chickering Moller.
    p. cm.
  Includes bibliographical references and index.
  ISBN 1-56308-719-7 (softbound)
  1. Hispanic Americans and libraries. 2. Public libraries--Services to Hispanic Americans. 3. Libraries--Special collections--Hispanic Americans. 4. Hispanic Americans--Information services. 5. Hispanic Americans--Library resources. 6. Hispanic Americans--Databases. I. Title.

Z711.8 .M65 2000
027.6'3--dc21
                                                              00-045090

Contents

Acknowledgments

Thanks go to the following people who took time to speak and/or correspond with me, and for sharing their expertise in providing library services for Spanish-speakers. My apologies to anyone I have forgotten to name.

Carolann Abramoff, Hudson (Fla.) Regional Library

Alma Flor Ada

Ernesto Almonte Escudero, Librarian, Iquique English College, Iquique, Chile

Amando Alvarez, Denver Public Library

Laurie Aude, Aurora (Ill.) Public Library

Sandra Ríos Balderrama, American Library Association

Toni Bissessar, Brooklyn Public Library

Beckie Brazell, Denver Public Library

Kathy Brendza, The Center, Leadville, Colo.

Larry Burgess, Redlands (Calif.) Public Library

Amanda Castillo, Tucson-Pima (Ariz.) Public Library System

Jeri Chavez, Lake Co. (Colo.) Public Schools

Jennifer Comi, San Antonio Public Library

Loraine Cors, Hudson (Fla.) Regional Library

Danelle Crowley, San Antonio Public Library

Maria DeHerrera, Conejos County (Colo.) Public Library

Luis del Castillo

Mary Ebuna, Colorado Mountain College

Beth Elder, Denver Public Library

Maritza Escobar Mamani, Librarian, Instituto Agrícola Kusayapu, Chile

Oralia Garza de Cortés

Peter Everett, Bridgeport (Conn.) Public Library

Christine Gonzalez, San Diego Public Library

Mary Ann Gonzalez, Hartford (Conn.) Public Library

Ramona Grijalva, Tucson-Pima (Ariz.) Public Library System

Tanya Hajjar, Montrose (Colo.) Public Library

Julie Herrera, Alamosa (Colo.) Public Schools

Nora Holmes, Alamosa (Colo.) High School

Catherine Jasper, School of Library and Information Science, University of South Florida

Stacey Reese Kelly, Lake Co. (Colo.) Public Schools

Lydia Kuhn, Fresno (Calif.) Public Library

Marsha Labodda, Del Valle High School Library, El Paso, Tex.

Melissa Leyte, Twombly School, Ft. Lupton, Colo.

Hector Marino, Formerly of Denver Public Schools

Rosalie Martinez, Former Principal, Margaret May Twombly School, Ft. Lupton, Colo.

Charlotte McKee, Saguache (Colo.) Public Library

Elissa Miller, Arlington Co. (Va.) Public Library

Teresa Mlawer, Lectorum

Sue Moore, Leo Wm. Butler Elementary School, Ft. Lupton, Colo.

Pat Mora

Diana Morales, Houston Public Library

Margaret Morris, Southern Peaks Public Library, Alamosa, Colo.

Jan Mustain-Wood, formerly of Fort Lupton Public and School Library, Ft. Lupton, Colo.

Ben Ocón, Salt Lake City Public Library

Margarita Ortiz, Detroit Public Library

Lucy Osius, The Center, Leadville, Colo.

Janet Oslund, Montrose (Colo.) Public Library

Elaine Pace, EBSCO

Irania Macías Patterson, Public Library of Charlotte & Mecklenberg County, N.C.

Linda Payne-Button, Our Lady of the Lake University, San Antonio, Tex.

Benjamín Pérez Ledesma

Verla Peterson, Branigan Library, Las Cruces, N.M.

Clara Rey, Tucumcari, N.M.

Carol Riggs, Littleton (Colo.) Public Schools

Ofelya Ramírez, Denver Public Library

Martín Rivera, Tucson-Pima (Ariz.) Public Library

Gloria Romero, Lake Co. (Colo.) Public Schools

Dr. Isabel Schon

Michael Shapiro, Libros Sin Fronteras

Mary Lee Smith, Lovington (N.M.) Public Library

Sue Struthers, Riverside (Calif.) Public Library

Jon Sundell, Forsyth County Public Library, Winston-Salem, N.C.

Becky Tatar, Aurora (Ill.) Public Library

Sandra Tauler, Camarena Memorial Library, Calexico, Calif.

Becky Tellez Pombo, Harriet Johnson Primary School, Tucson, Ariz.

Rose Treviño, San Antonio Public Library

Guadalupe Uquillas, Pontifical Catholic University of Ecuador in Quito

Elaine Valenzuela, Tucson-Pima (Ariz.) Public Library System

Zoraya Vázquez, Saguache (Colo.) Public Library

Gabriela Wheeler, Denver Public Library

Cherie White

And to Bruce for the inspiration.

Preface

Work on this book has shown me that there is considerable expertise in this country on providing library services to Spanish-speakers (and other language minorities), but that the information is scattered and somewhat difficult to access without effort. I have certainly not provided answers for every question, and in many cases there is no single answer. In some cases I have only helped identify the questions that need to be addressed. It is my hope that this book will be a compilation of the best of the advice and pertinent questions, and will serve as a springboard to those librarians and library staff new to this journey.

Although the emphasis is on Spanish-language resources, some of the materials listed would also be appropriate for English-speakers of Latino heritage seeking to reconnect with their cultural roots, or for any students wishing to learn about Latino cultures. In most cases I have not tried to recommend specific titles because Isabel Schon and others have done that previously. Instead, I have attempted to provide general guidelines so librarians can choose material and services best suited to their specific patrons.

After my initial experience in Latin America I have felt an affinity for the area and its people, and this is an attempt to reciprocate for the valuable life lessons I have learned.

My special thanks go to Jean Parry and Nancy McCain who offered encouragement and assistance, to Colorado Mountain College that allowed me a flexible schedule to be able to research and write this book, and to my personal technical advisors: Jim French, Gary Cummings, and Steve Voynick.

Introduction

Shortly after we were married in the early 1970s, my husband, Pete, swept me over 6,000 miles from home to live in rural south central Chile for three years. It wasn't a surprise – I knew his career aspirations before he even proposed marriage and was looking forward to the adventure. What did surprise me, however, was the culture shock that devastated me, especially during our three months of language study in Cuernavaca, Mexico. The adjustments to a new husband in a new culture with a new language took their toll. I must have cried nearly every day — part of me anxious to learn to communicate in Spanish, another part fighting the whole way. The great amount of change in such a short time period sometimes overwhelmed me, even though I was an eager participant.

For those three years in Chile I experienced, to some extent, what it was like: being in the minority; struggling with understanding and being understood in a new language; trying to take in and process, daily, new sights, sounds, and cultural mores; knowing that people were talking politics, but not understanding whether they were for or against the particular issue; and living through political upheaval that tore a society apart. I was forced to put aside "truths" I had always taken for granted and become more adaptable. Despite those frustrating challenges, I can now say the experience was enriching and well worth the effort. I came to appreciate that there are many different perspectives on life— all equally valid, depending on one's circumstances, prior experiences, and beliefs.

Today, as a librarian in a community experiencing a large influx of Mexican nationals arriving to work in the ski industry, I have a better understanding of what these families must be going through. Anyone who has been uprooted from familiar surroundings to relocate in a totally new environment, even one that promises a better life, will experience stress and anxiety. For children who may not have been involved in the decision, the move may seem even more incomprehensible and frightening. I can thoroughly understand the relief I see in people's faces when I speak to them in Spanish and can appreciate why Spanish-speakers are more inclined to visit my library when I am there rather than approach other staff members who speak little or no Spanish.

Constantly having to concentrate on how to express oneself in an unfamiliar language is taxing. It is not just a matter of remembering how to substitute a word from one language for that of another. Rather, it is a matter of learning a whole new way of processing thought, a different way of viewing the world. You may know the question you wish to ask, but not have the vocabulary or syntax to ask it. You feel stupid, lacking in intelligence. It can be demoralizing— like a bad dream in which you try to scream, but no sound comes out.

It will probably always be a struggle for me to express myself adequately, with all the necessary nuances, in Spanish, even though I have made subsequent trips to Mexico, Costa Rica, Chile, Ecuador, Bolivia, and Peru where I have practiced the language. I still do not automatically pick up leisure reading in Spanish—it has to be a conscious decision because I am much more comfortable and skilled reading English—my native language. So, I can empathize with Latinos who are feeling similar frustrations in reverse.

■ Leadville, Colorado

Our small, isolated community of Leadville, Colorado, is fortunate to have three professional librarians: Jean Parry, Lake County School District Library Coordinator; Nancy McCain, Director of the Lake County Public Library; and myself, Director of the Learning Resources Center of Timberline Campus, Colorado Mountain College. As friends and colleagues, we work together closely to try to maximize the library resources available to our public. The collections in each of our libraries are open to anyone in the community, as well as to patrons of libraries across the state who participate in the Colorado Library Card program, and through interlibrary loan. In 1992, Jean Parry began to agonize over ways her libraries (elementary, middle, and high schools) could serve the increasing numbers of monolingual Spanish-speaking students enrolling in the school district.

Through a number of brainstorming sessions we began to formulate a plan that included seeking grant funding to purchase Spanish language materials for our libraries. Our very first cooperative grant-writing attempt was successful, and we have since written other successful cooperative grants. We did not consider ourselves experts, but by combining our expertise, seeking assistance from other members of our community, and much trial and error, we have developed some strategies to try to begin serving our Spanish-speaking clientele. Though none of us is Latina, we hope that with empathy and open minds we can avoid the stereotypical attitudes we hear around us and focus on the real needs of this population.

At the beginning of our efforts, little literature was available on library service for monolingual Spanish library users, but we were lucky to be successful using the hunt and seek method. We stumbled on a few suppliers and prevailed on friends (mostly teachers) traveling to Mexico and Central America during vacations to pick up books that looked good, then branched out from there. Much of the literature available in the United States is aimed at the patron of Latino descent who is already somewhat acculturated to the United States, and speaks and reads some English.

But the questions still remained: How does the public or school librarian or media specialist with limited Spanish language even begin to meet the needs of a population with limited or no English skills? Where does one turn for help in selecting suitable materials, especially materials for children and young adults?

What kinds of resources are available to help ameliorate cultural clashes between students from Latino and non-Latino cultures?

These were the questions I tried to keep in mind as I began to work on this book, the research for which really began in 1992 although I didn't realize it then.

■ Why Bilingual Resources?

I often hear people express the opinion: "If those Mexicans are coming to the United States to work, they better learn English. Why should we cater to them in Spanish?"

In 1998, California voters approved Proposition 227, which essentially replaced bilingual education in that state with a program of intensive instruction in English. Two years later a newspaper headline proclaimed: "Test scores improve after bilingual ban: Spanish-speaking students in Calif. immersed in English." (Steinberg, 20 Aug. 2000). Only briefly mentioned is the fact that classroom sizes were reduced over the same time period, another factor that could account for the improved scores.

Although on the surface immersing students in the language seems to have improved their English skills, only long-term research and experience can assess the true outcome. However, in the meantime, voters in other states are being tempted to pass similar initiatives on the basis of the inconclusive California results. If, as a result of such actions, school libraries are forced to curtail collection development in languages other than English, it will be imperative for public libraries to take up that slack because the need for informational materials in those languages will not diminish.

Statistics from the U.S. Census Bureau estimate that the Hispanic population in the United States will nearly double between the years 2000 and 2025 (from 31 million to nearly 59 million). As shown in the first chapter of this book, Latino young people (those born in the United States and those from other countries) are more likely to be undereducated than any other ethnic group in this country (Carrasquillo 1991, 93). Some of the reasons for this will also be discussed in Chapter 3 and Chapter 5. Any investment in appropriate Spanish-language materials by libraries would be an investment in the future. Despite English-only proponents, use of the Spanish language is not going to decrease in the United States in the foreseeable future.

Although progress in adapting to the United States may not be as speedy as some would like, eliminating programs that will ultimately help immigrants succeed makes little sense. Educators I spoke with expressed the opinion that the pendulum of public argument periodically swings between English-only and bilingual education. Eventually public sentiment will again espouse bilingualism, but in the meantime many students may not get the basics they need.

Recent research in bilingual education indicates that a strong foundation in one's first language is necessary to succeed in learning a second. Sosa (1993, 13) reported that minority, working-class children are more apt to be deficient in language skills when their first language is of low prestige in the majority of society's eyes and they feel forced to learn in the foreign, majority language. If we can encourage students to remain fluent in their first language and give them the tools to do so, they will be better able to succeed in English and will retain a skill (ability to speak Spanish) that could serve them well in the future.

While immigrant children struggle with English, their education in other areas does not stop. Just because they stumble over English or never ask questions does not mean they are lacking in intellectual ability. If they are stymied in learning what is being expected of them in a timely fashion, perhaps, instead, they will learn things educators would rather not have them learn: that school is too hard, that nothing relevant is being taught, that there isn't any use trying, that no one understands them.

From my own experiences, I know that learning a foreign language and studying in that language are not easy. Studies have shown that although limited-English-proficient (LEP) students can become proficient in conversational English within two years, it can take six or more years to develop the skills needed for academic success (Cummins 1993, 12). Students who have difficulty understanding, speaking, reading, or writing English are considered to be LEP.

Studies by the Colorado State Library and Adult Education Office have shown that "the size of a library media center's staff and collection is the best school predictor of academic achievement" (Lance 1992). Logically, this would be as true for Spanish-speaking students as for speakers of any other language. Library resources in Spanish would therefore help Latino students learn the fundamental concepts being introduced in the curriculum, bridge gaps in understanding, integrate new material into their current knowledge base, and ultimately achieve more success academically and in life. Spanish-language resources should not be seen as merely supplemental library materials, but as integral parts of collections serving Latino populations.

Today, with the ease with which people cross national boundaries for employment, business, or vacation, we need to encourage greater understanding of cultural values, similarities, and differences. Here in Colorado, for instance, multilingual employees working for Japanese-owned ski resorts catering to Mexican tourists should be in high demand. In this information age, that international scenario will become more and more familiar in all types of business and industry, and we need to be preparing students for such a world.

This book is especially aimed at the librarian-media specialist who recognizes the value of bilingual-bicultural education and is looking for ideas in meeting the challenge of serving Spanish-speaking patrons.

◼ Works Cited

Carrasquillo, Angela L. *Hispanic Children and Youth in the United States: A Resource Guide.* New York: Garland, 1991.

Cummins, Jim. Empowerment Through Biliteracy. In *The Power of Two Languages: Literacy and Biliteracy for Spanish-Speaking Students,* edited by Josefina Villamil Tinajero and Alma Flor Ada. New York: Macmillan McGraw-Hill School Publishing, 1993.

Lance, Keith Curry, Lynda Wellborn, and Christine Hamilton-Pennell. *The Impact of School Library Media Centers on Academic Achievement.* Denver: Colorado Dept. of Education, 1992.

Sosa, Alicia. *Thorough and Fair: Creating Routes to Success for Mexican-American Students.* Charleston, W.Va.: 1993. ERIC Clearinghouse on Rural Education and Small Schools, 1993.

Steinberg, Jacques. "Test Scores Improve After Bilingual Ban." *The Denver Post*, 20 August 2000.

Chapter 1

Understanding the History

■ From the Beginning

Apart from the languages of Native American peoples, Spanish was the first language to be introduced into the New World. By the early 16th century explorers, *conquistadores,* and Christian missionaries sailing under the flag of maritime power, Spain, had explored the entire Atlantic coast of the Americas. Their presence was most strongly felt, however, in areas of the Caribbean, Mexico, South America, and the U.S. Southwest. As the native peoples were decimated by disease, warfare, and intermarriage, Spanish became the dominant Old World language in use.

With time, English-speaking peoples began to dominate the eastern seaboard and the Spanish gained control in Mexico, with their sphere of influence spreading north into Texas, California, Utah, and Nevada as well as parts of Arizona, Colorado, New Mexico, Kansas, Oklahoma, and Wyoming (Shorris 1992, 39). The distance from the political hub in Mexico City, hostilities from native peoples, and a band of barren desert complicated communication, and the Spaniards and subsequently the Mexicans never held tight control over these northern territories. Influence lessened as settlers and adventurers from the United States ventured west, and eventually the United States began to claim these areas as its own.

Following the Mexican-American War of 1846–1848, the Treaty of Guadalupe Hidalgo ceded much of this disputed territory to the United States for a payment of $15 million. Residents of the ceded area were given a choice of returning to Mexican territory or remaining where they were and becoming U.S. citizens. The majority decided to stay. Spanish-speaking people who had lived in the area for two to three centuries and were remote from the seats of government saw no apparent reason to give up speaking their familiar tongue, nor their family ties, culture, habits, or ways of thinking and being. The border was still fluid and it probably made little difference in which country they resided. Residents who remained had not crossed the border, rather "the border crossed us" (Shorris 1992, 37).

Whether by accident or design, the United States has continued to involve itself in the affairs of its Spanish-speaking neighbors into the twentieth century. For example, the United States occupied Cuba from 1898–1902; encouraged an insurrection in Panama in 1903 that led to its independence from Colombia and subsequently allowed the United States to build the Panama Canal; sent U.S. Marines to occupy Nicaragua from 1912–1925 and 1926–1933; during the 1950s, helped overthrow the government of Guatemala to protect U.S. business interests; sent troops to the Dominican Republic in 1965, ostensibly because Communists had infiltrated pro-government forces; and in the early 1970s, helped destabilize the democratically elected government of Chilean President Salvador Allende.

After such a long history of involvement with Spanish-speaking peoples, it should be no surprise that the United States is destined to continue those relationships into the twenty-first century, hopefully with more positive motivations and results than some of its past endeavors.

■ The People

Because of the proximity of Mexico to the United States and the discrepancy of per capita incomes between these two nations, it is understandable that the largest number of immigrants into the United States from any country today are from Mexico—more than one-fourth of all foreign-born residents according to the Latin American Research and Service Agency (LARASA) (May 1997). Who can fault Mexicans for this situation, when the U.S. government as well as private business encourage immigration when the economy is good (i.e., a cheap source of labor for jobs few others want)? Unfortunately, when the economy sours, deportations are stepped up and people are expected to go back from where they came.

The Mexican-born population in the United States tends to be young: 59 percent of them are under age 35 and 13 percent are 18 or under (LARASA May 1997). Traditionally, Mexicans were less likely than other immigrants to participate in the political process in this country because they did not see their stay in the United States as permanent (Gann and Duignan 1986, 43–47). More recently, however, Mexico has changed its policies to allow for dual citizenship, so Mexicans who obtain U.S. citizenship can still be fully repatriated at any time.

We can hope Mexicans will now feel more empowered to work toward change that benefits them economically and politically here in the United States because they do not have to renounce their Mexican nationality to do so (Mendosa 1998).

Smaller populations have migrated from the Dominican Republic, and Central and South America—especially Colombia, Ecuador, and Peru, but taken together they form about 14 percent of the Spanish-speaking population or the second largest group in the United States. Central Americans are concentrated in California, Texas, Florida, Illinois, New York, and the Washington, D.C. areas, with growing communities in Seattle, Denver, and Boston; Ecuadorians tend to head for New Jersey (Hispanic Business March 1998, 16). When countries suffer varying degrees of political oppression and/or economic hardship, their citizens feel forced to seek better lives elsewhere, and the prosperity of the United States always beckons.

Approximately 12 percent or 2.7 million Hispanics are Puerto Ricans. It is now estimated that two-fifths of all Puerto Ricans live on the mainland (Mestre and Nieto 1996). Since the end of the fifteenth century, the people of the island have been a conquered people, becoming a U.S. possession in 1899 following the Spanish-American War (Shorris 1992, 223). As ease of travel improved and social conditions and unemployment rates on the island worsened by the late 1940s, more and more Puerto Ricans migrated to the mainland, eventually concentrating primarily in New York, New Jersey, and southern New England. They faced no quotas, as did other populations, because they had been granted citizenship. As with Mexicans, travel between the "home country" and the mainland is easy, so cultural, familial, and linguistic ties continue to be maintained. However, Puerto Ricans are part of a double bind: officially part of the United States, they still often are considered an immigrant cultural minority (Romberg 1996, 16).

Cubans, who in the late 1950s and early 1960, envisioned a temporary political exile from the regime of Fidel Castro in Dade County, Florida, may find that they have created a permanent community-in-exile as older generations pass away, and the younger people have no first-hand knowledge of the Caribbean homeland. With Castro's inevitable demise within the near future, the situation of Cuban-Americans will be interesting to note. However, it is safe to say that, as the fourth largest Latino minority in the United States, the Cuban-Americans will not go away. If and when travel restrictions are relaxed, they, like the Mexicans and Puerto Ricans, will be able to easily renew cultural and business ties, but will undoubtedly return to the States where they have established homes and economic security. Of the Latino populations that have migrated to the United States, the Cubans, especially those who arrived in the early years of Castro's dictatorship, tend to be the most well-educated and the most well-off financially.

As the Hispanic-origin population in the United States continues to grow into the new century, communities are springing up in unexpected places, not just in the traditional cities of Miami, San Antonio, Los Angeles, and New York. Hispanics can now be found working in areas that have not typically had strong

Latino populations such as in grain elevators in Kansas, on tobacco and horse farms in Kentucky, or in restaurant and construction firms in North Carolina. No longer are Latinos employed mainly as migrant farm workers in the Southwest or Midwest anymore. Less than 8 percent of the Hispanic population is involved in farming, forestry, and fishing, although in those industries, more Mexicans are employed than any other nationality.

Although periodic reports in the news media would have us believe that undocumented immigrants are swarming over the country, the Urban Institute estimated in 1992 that they actually amounted to only 1.3 percent of the total U.S. population (LARASA January 1995). It should be no surprise then, that with 500 years of an intermingled history, the U.S. Census Bureau estimated a population of over 30 million people of Hispanic origin as of March 1998 with projections of 96.5 million for the year 2050 (U.S. Bureau of Census April 30, 1998; Statistical Abstract, Table 13).

Hispanic, Latino, Chicano, Spanish-American?

It would be nice to have one generic term to refer to our Spanish-speaking or Spanish-heritage population, but it is not that simple. First, as the U.S. Census Bureau at last recognizes, people of Hispanic background (the term chosen by the U.S. government) may be of any race. This book will use *Spanish-speaking* most frequently as that is the common element of the people targeted for library service.

Until the late 1920s, most of the native population in the Southwest (especially New Mexico and Texas) referred to themselves as Mexicans, because that was their ancestral heritage. However, with a new influx of Mexican immigrants, those who had been here a while wished to be distinguished from the newcomers and began using such terms as Spanish-Americans or Latin-Americans for themselves. As with other groups of people, the name by which they prefer to be called changes with the times, the underlying political climate, and current social connotations.

Hispanic derives from the word *Hispania*, the Latin name for the Iberian Peninsula (Spain and Portugal). The main objection Spanish-speaking people have to the use of *Hispanic* is that it does not recognize any of the other ethnic or racial groups that have gone into the makeup of different peoples—only the heritage from Spain. This is the term currently used by the U.S. Census Bureau and appears to be more prevalent on the East Coast (Cuello 1996).

Latino originates in Latin America, and refers to those parts of North and South America (except Canada) where one of the Romance languages (French, Spanish, or Portuguese) is spoken. People who use this term feel it is more inclusive, and has less of a connotation of Spanish colonialism.

Chicano is a term used mainly for people of Mexican descent, especially those who were born in the United States (to distinguish from those who immigrated more recently from Mexico). Once a derogatory term used for the lower classes, or by the working classes to refer to themselves, *Chicano* was adopted by the California Mexican-American student civil rights movement in the late 1960s to apply to themselves as social activists (McWilliams 1990, 355; Acuña 1988, 338).

And, to add to the number of names used by different Latino groups, *Nuyoricans* refers to Puerto Ricans who live on the mainland. For Puerto Ricans wanting to de-emphasize the colonized status of the island, *Boricuas*, derived from *Borinquen*, the indigenous name of the island, is sometimes used (Cuello 1996).

It is a mistake to feel the needs of the entire Hispanic/Latino population can all be met in the same ways. In assessing the information needs of longer term residents versus newcomers, it is best to treat them as separate populations. There may be some overlap, but try not to let "old-timers" feel you are neglecting them to serve the newer immigrants. However, some of the been-here-for-a-generation-or-more population, especially those who still fully appreciate the Spanish language and heritage, can be some of your best allies and may be able to serve as liaisons to the newer residents.

In our community we have found there is probably more of a cultural clash between Latinos who are longer term U.S. residents and for whom English is the first language, and the new Latin American immigrants, than there is between non-Latinos and either of those two groups. These tensions may be especially evident among teenagers who are struggling with identity issues. Inevitably, any new immigrant group starts out at the bottom of the social ladder, which elevates people on this social ladder up a rung or two. People who are no longer at the bottom do not wish to be identified with those who are, and tend to be defensive about their new social position. For the same reasons that people of the Southwest stopped referring to themselves as Mexicans in the 1920s, Latinos today who have "paid their dues" want to be considered full-fledged members of U.S. society and do not want to be confused with immigrants.

In deciding what to call anyone, it is best to follow that person's lead. Many may prefer to be known by their country of origin—Chileans or Mexicans or Peruvians. Or, even better, refer to them by name (but try to get the pronunciation reasonably correct). Isn't that the best way to refer to any of us rather than trying to lump many unique individuals into one impersonal category?

Cultural Characteristics

Although there is a risk in attempting to explain Latinos, of implying that they are all alike or of perpetuating misleading stereotypes, I would like to explain some traits that tend to be true for many Latinos, to assist with an understanding of their cultures. To emphasize further, however, each Latino community, and indeed each individual within that community, is different from another depending on such factors as national origin, social class and income, levels of acculturation and education, and language ability (in Spanish, English, or other indigenous tongues) (LARASA March 1997). Have the person's forebears been living around Santa Fe since 1700? Was the family head a college professor or successful entrepreneur who left Cuba when Castro came into power? Or did the peasant family recently come from Guatemala in fear of bodily harm or death?

Two characteristics that do hold for all Latinos are the Spanish language and the heritage of the Spanish Conquest. Unlike the Puritans and others who settled along the Atlantic shore of North America for reasons of political and religious freedom, the Spaniards came as conquerors, looking for avenues to power and wealth through discoveries of land and mineral resources. The legacy they left was one of exploitation of land and people rather than of settlement and agricultural enterprise. Much of how the Latin peoples think of themselves today has come from whether they identified more with the conquered or the conquerors—the exploited or the exploiters.

Accompanying the conquering Spaniards were clergy looking to convert souls to Roman Catholicism, although some also sought to secure their own share of power and wealth. With its strict social codes, the Church taught loyalty and obedience to authority—lessons the majority of people learned all too well. For women, the lessons evolved into the tradition of pleasing others and working to meet their needs (especially those of husbands and children) before tending to one's own needs. Although Protestantism and Pentecostalism have now established footholds in Latin American countries, the legacy of Catholicism and other entrenched "Christian" values remains.

Immediate and extended family relationships are important to Latinos and are based on interdependence and cooperation. One's sense of self-pride and worth comes from being part of a family group. For that reason, it is understandable that as people migrate to a new country they tend to settle in areas with others from their same country or region who understand their language and cultural heritage, and with whom they can establish essential support networks (Carrasquillo 1991, 51; LARASA March 1997; Shorris 1992, 218).

Latinos are much more openly warm and affectionate than we reserved Yankees. When I visited my 20-year-old daughter the year she was studying in Ecuador, it was nice to be able to walk down the street holding hands with her—something she had not let me do for years at home, but nevertheless a sign of the affection we feel for each other. In a family or group setting, it is expected that as each person arrives and later departs, they will circle the room, individually greeting each person with at least a handshake, but often with an embrace and a kiss—even men may embrace each other heartily. I find this a much friendlier custom than just giving a general greeting from the doorway or middle of the room.

Good manners in Latino cultures call for a person to be nonconfrontational and to not look the other person directly in the eye. While the truth may be many different things depending on one's outlook or point of view, Latinos are more likely to tell you what they think you want to hear, or fabricate an answer rather than admit they do not know or disappoint you with the wrong answer. It is rather along the same lines as we Anglos who tell little white lies or fudge the truth to avoid hurting someone's feelings. Similarly, parents and children have been taught respect for teachers. This may make young children more obedient students than some of their non-Latino classmates, but may also mean parents are less inclined to speak with teachers when there are problems, feeling that teachers, as authority figures, know best.

Families

As noted earlier, families are an important social unit in Latin cultures. Older children are more likely to live with parents until they marry, and parents (grandparents) often live with their adult children. In traditional societies this arrangement provided more help in caring for children, the elderly, and/or disabled. In poverty-stricken areas, however, child care may fall to a slightly older sibling, or the mother may have all her young children accompany her as she tries to make a living selling merchandise on the street.

The woman's role has traditionally been within the household and she has been held in high esteem for her abilities to care for the domestic needs of the family and supervise the upbringing of the children, including their religious education. It has been interesting for me to see the support women give each other on an Ecuadorian bus or in an English as a Second Language (ESL) class in this country. On more than one occasion I have seen a woman automatically pick up a friend's toddler who had been sitting on its mother's lap when that mother needed to nurse her infant. Most women (from whatever culture) want a better life for their children than they themselves had, want to have pride in their children and their accomplishments, and want the children to have a better education than they did. As is true in this country, however, more and more women are finding it necessary to seek employment outside the home to supplement family income, so must relegate child care to another person or agency.

Studies show that Latinas in the United States tend to marry younger, have larger families, and stay in relationships longer than women of other ethnic groups. They are also poorer and have less education, both of which will be explored in more detail later. Domestic violence occurs in families of all social and economic levels, and Latino women are probably no more prone to be victims than any other group of immigrant women. However, a report by the LARASA details some of the problems they do face (April 1998).

New immigrants have to deal with stress associated with such factors as: acculturation, underemployment, undereducation, economic pressures, isolation, and the shift of their children's values away from traditional ones. In some cases families are divided when some children have been left in the home country with relatives, and others have accompanied parents to this country. The more stressors a family experiences, the more inclined members are to try to rigidly recreate traditional values, unable or afraid to allow for accommodations that must be made for the new environment. Women, pressured by their men and by values about the sanctity of marriage and family that have been engrained in them, feel obligated to preserve families at all costs. Domestic violence may then result from conflicts involved in trying to enforce "traditional" family values when some family members, especially children, may be picking up the seemingly contradictory values of the dominant society. (LARASA April 1998).

To add to pressures facing Latino families, Shorris (1992, 44–47) explains that Mexican workers (and most likely other Latinos as well) have been manipulated by employers and others to devalue the worth of their labor, forcing them, because of internal pride and stoicism to provide for their family, to work two or three low-paying jobs to try to make ends meet. Although they are doing their best to provide for the family's material needs, they inadvertently contribute to the breakdown of the family unit because they no longer have time to spend with the family.

Socioeconomic Factors

Many Latin Americans see the United States as a utopia, and in many respects it is, compared to the conditions they endured in their home country. Because wages are higher in the United States, many Latinos are willing to put up with conditions that many of the rest of us would not consider: two or three jobs (that no one else wants), overcrowded living conditions (because it's easier to share the rent among several people), no health insurance, few prospects for job advancement, and no unemployment insurance or Workman's Compensation. U.S. Census statistics show that immigrants who arrived during the 1990s are more likely to live in poverty, have lower income levels, and higher unemployment rates than natural-born citizens. However, their economic circumstances do improve with length of residence and citizenship. Immigrants (from all nations) who arrived during the 1970s are now doing as well income-wise as the native-born (U.S. Bureau of Census, April 1997).

Latino-origin persons are more likely to be found in occupations such as operators, fabricators, laborers, and service providers than the population as a whole (43 percent versus 27.6 percent). Although, according to U.S. Census Bureau Statistics from March 1996, Puerto Ricans had the highest unemployment rate (10.8 percent) and the highest number living below the poverty level (38.1 percent), Mexicans had the lowest median earnings for those employed full-time ($19,028 for men, $15,998 for women). Cuban-Americans tend to be the more financially successful of the Latinos with 37.4 percent of the employed making $25,000 to $49,999 and only 6.2 percent unemployed. Those from Central and South America fall in the middle of the above categories—neither doing the best nor the worst (U.S. Bureau of Census, February 1998).

A director of social services for a Colorado county in the middle of the ski resort area gave examples of some of the exploitation that often results for Latino workers: "Tourism drives Colorado. The state won't allow us to do anything to kill the sacred cow. . . . If the INS (Immigration & Naturalization Service) did its job and deported every illegal, the (ski) resort and construction industries would shut down the same day. . . . It's all economics." This director also reported instances of undocumented employees working up to four weeks for construction firms, only to be let go just before payday. Because they have no documents, they have no legal recourse (Chickering 1997, 16). Surely the employer is at least as much to blame as the employee.

Education

Latinos, with the largest school-age minority population, have the lowest level of education of any group within the United States. This includes persons in the United States for whom English is the first language, as well as immigrants who are more comfortable thinking and speaking in Spanish or another language. Although 53 percent of Latinos aged 25 and over have at least a high school diploma, they have the highest dropout rate (between 30 and 35 percent) and tend to drop out at an earlier age—40 percent before completing the ninth grade (Facts on Hispanics, Feb. 1998; *Our Nation on the Fault Line,* 1996; U.S. Bureau of Census, April 1997). Seventy percent of Mexican-born immigrants are not high school graduates, nor are 47 percent of those who reside in Puerto Rico (LARASA May 1997; *Our Nation on the Fault Line,* 1996).

A Latino woman educator who grew up in Colorado explained that as late as the 1950s, school officials were encouraging Latino students to drop out at the end of the seventh or eighth grades to work in the fields (Martinez 1998). With this difficult-to-overcome historic legacy, it is no wonder Latinos remain undereducated.

Children whose families have few or no successful educational experiences are at risk before they begin school. Immigrant parents may not be aware of the skills and experiences children need to prepare them for school, and may not themselves have strong verbal skills in any language to pass on. Because a good foundation in one's first language is necessary for success in learning a second, these children are at a distinct disadvantage from the very beginning.

Carrasquillo (1991, 87–95) believed that minority students are at risk just by living in the United States. When limited-English-proficient (LEP) students enter school they may be faced with a threatening (to them) environment and culture, in a language they struggle to understand, if they understand it at all. Racism may be subtle, but institutionalized, as when we expect less of Latino children, fail to respect their "unusual" customs and beliefs, or offer library books in which the heroes are always white men and boys.

Often of a lower socioeconomic level, the Latino family may live in a poorer neighborhood with fewer resources to provide a quality education in the schools. Teachers who see social differences as educational deficiencies may not recognize the previous language and culture of the Latino student as resources to enrich the entire classroom. Because their language skills are lacking, and because much of classroom teaching/learning depends on listening and speaking skills, students may be perceived as having a learning disability. Even if classrooms do not offer bilingual educational opportunities, school and public libraries can assist by offering appropriate Spanish-language materials and taking many opportunities to celebrate the richness of the culture(s).

■ Latin American Schools, Libraries, and Books

In trying to develop library services for the Spanish-speaking members of our community, my colleague librarians and I wondered about their previous library experiences, if any. So, on my past few trips to Mexico, Ecuador, and specifically Chile, I made attempts to visit libraries and question Latino friends about their own library use. The following descriptions and impressions may not be universally true, but will give some general ideas of what libraries and education are like in Latin American countries.

In Latin America, private schools (K–12 equivalents) are much more common than in the United States. Only the poorest students attend the government-funded public schools.

Mexico

The Mexican school system is divided into six years of *primaria*, three years of *secundaria* (equivalent to middle school), and three years of *preparatoria* (senior high). Until very recently, only the first nine years were considered as part of a basic education. At the successful completion of 12 years, students receive a *Bachillerato*, which equates to a high school diploma, not a university baccalaureate degree. The degree given at the end of university study is a *Licenciatura*. According to a Mexican seminarian serving an internship in our community, most students do not begin to take studying seriously until they get to the senior high level; however, many have previously dropped out. Although there are libraries in public schools, students are more likely to view a class trip to the library as a fun outing rather than a period for research or instruction. Public libraries are viewed as places to get together with friends to "shoot the breeze," with maybe a little studying on the side.

For those who can afford to purchase reading material, there are newsstands selling magazines, newspapers, and paperback books on nearly every street corner in Mexico. Or, if one were interested, one could at least stand and read the headlines without purchasing anything. But for the majority of Mexicans who work hard to scrape by, reading is not a high priority.

A friend in Mexico City who is Dean of Students at a theological seminary says: "[My two teenage] boys basically do research at home with all the books and encyclopedias that we have, plus the Internet now. Also, even though the teachers ask for some research projects, they don't seem to be too demanding and [the boys] get by with those resources" (White 1998).

During a study trip to Cuernavaca in 1995, I visited the Seventeenth of April Library after seeing a poster indicating that free guided tours were offered. The salmon-colored building fronted with colorful murals had first opened in April 1994 and sat in the middle of the park-like setting in a newer, more affluent suburb. Teenagers on in-line skates whizzed past. To one side was a smaller, brand-new children's library that was to open shortly with books, games, videos and computers.

Entering the main door, I passed a guard and left my pack in the checkroom because no bags or packages were allowed inside. Students were required to sign in (name, age, school grade) so library staff had an indication of who their clientele was. The book stacks were "open" and classified with Dewey call numbers. Patrons could find their own selections using a manual card catalog. At that time materials could not leave the library although the staff anticipated checkout would be possible at some point in the future. Pages from books in the general collection could be photocopied, but not those in the reference collection because the photocopying process was too damaging to book spines.

I was visiting on a Friday in midafternoon and found the many tables occupied by groups of elementary and high school aged students. Many of 25,000 book volumes were duplicate copies and appeared to be geared to the needs of students. There were very few magazines or newspapers and I did not find any popular new fiction titles such as *Como Agua Para Chocolate* or novels by Isabel Allende. Instead the collection contained classics like *Uncle Tom's Cabin* and a book about Helen Keller (both in Spanish)—the types of books one might expect to study for a class assignment rather than for enjoyment or personal improvement.

Open seven days a week, the library also had a collection of 200–300 videotapes, which could be viewed in-house. During my visit, three schoolboys had pulled chairs close to the television and were watching a video on how to speak English. Special programming included story hours for children up to 12 years of age, literary gatherings, reading and painting workshops, theater and/or interpretive readings, a map room, and special displays.

Another day in the nearby town of Tepotzlán I saw a sign painted on the side of a building: *LEER ES BUENA COSTUMBRE. VISITA TU BIBLIOTECA PUBLICA* (Reading is a good habit. Visit your public library).

Ecuador

Ecuador may be one of the poorer South American countries, but the Ecuadorians are warm and friendly, and the country is known for its wealth of natural beauty. Nevertheless, the resources available for libraries and books are even fewer than in Mexico. When a country has many social needs, books, unfortunately, tend to fall to the bottom of the priority list.

When asked about public education and libraries, an instructor at the Catholic University in Quito wrote:

> The lack of resources for public education means there is little
> money for books. The situation would vary in private schools. . . .
> A public school teacher surely would not have access to teach-
> ing materials, much less books. An instructor in a private
> school, however, has access to all the teaching materials neces-
> sary. Private schools have libraries with books not only in
> Spanish but English also. But in the latter case we would be
> speaking of an elite that in no way represents the majority of
> people. (Uquillas 1998, my translation)

When I asked about teaching methods, I was told (by a U.S. college student studying in the country): "One of the problems with education here is that students aren't supposed to ask questions. . . . If I ask a question (in Spanish class), the answer is often 'because that's the way it is. . . .' All that matters is the points you get on exams."

The Pontifical Catholic University of Ecuador, located in Quito, has one of the best libraries in the country, and like libraries everywhere in Latin American countries is hindered by low budgets and salaries. Library hours are 7 AM to 9 PM, Monday through Friday, with no weekend hours. Although the library is open to the public, only registered students may actually borrow materials. Books are checked out for a week and are renewable indefinitely if no one else requests them. Daily fines are charged for overdue materials, with the money going for materials' binding.

When I visited in early 1998, the collection had been automated for seven or eight years. However, with only three public access computers (soon to be increased to six), students still used the traditional card catalog. The library had a staff of 28, including maintenance personnel. Circulation was the largest department and included two staff people whose job it was to retrieve materials from the closed stacks. The most common way for students to do research was to submit subject requests that library staff searched. Students were then presented with printouts of relevant citations from which they made their selections. The periodical room, with 1,600 titles of which 400 were purchased and the remaining were gifts, had been open-access at one time. However, because of the loss rate the room is now closed and the only way to secure periodical articles is to present the citations and have the staff photocopy the articles. Enforcement of any copyright laws is lax at best. My understanding was that the supplier of the photocopy machines provided an employee to make the copies—at the equivalent of three cents per page, they would have to do a lot of business to make any kind of profit.

Chile

Iquique English College in this northern Chilean city is not a college in our sense of the word, but a prestigious church-run school for kindergarten through grade 14, with university-level classes offered in the evenings. The head librarian indicates the following about his school library:

> Our school has a library that is used by preschoolers, primary and intermediate students which are the different levels of education at the school. We also have students of higher education from I.E.C. Institute which functions nightly in the same building. Our library is used primarily as a reading room, for check-outs, and also for a story hour for preschoolers and students in first through fourth grades.
>
> At the beginning of the year, all classes visit the library and are given a talk on library use by the head librarian. They are taught the order of the book stands, use of the catalog, and requirements for checking out books, with emphasis on the help library staff can give them.
>
> Our library is scheduled for the implementation of computer equipment this year, to access Internet and automate the collection. . . . The other school and public libraries in Iquique do not have Internet access but some have computer equipment for automation. The library at the Arturo Prat University of Iquique does have an automated system and Internet access.
>
> Our library has open shelves. The use of open shelves is being promoted throughout Chile for school and public libraries, but most (libraries) do not have adequate personnel, infrastructure or appropriate equipment. Very few Chilean libraries use open shelves.
>
> The majority of libraries in Iquique lend out books to their students and teachers. In our school we have a system of *socios lectores*, but only in the area of literature. (Almonte 1998, my translation)

Socios lectores are community members who have cards to borrow from the school library, but they are restricted from borrowing any technical, professional books that would presumably be needed in direct support of educational programs.

A second librarian wrote of her experience at Instituto Agrícola Kusayapu, a boarding school in a rural region of northern Chile. Because there is no public library, her library is the only such resource in the area. Students may take materials to their dorm rooms, but those who live close enough to stay at home must leave their library cards with library staff when they check out materials.

> The use of the LRC [Learning Resources Center] Library is very constant since the Educational Reform requires the student to accomplish certain learning activities such as the following:

- The student uses the library to complete homework, for research projects, etc.
- During recreational periods, students can play games such as chess, checkers, dominoes and cards.
- The student can also view documentary or entertainment videos during free periods.
- The student uses the library during obligatory study periods at night—usually silent reading.

> The teachers coordinate the use of the room with the librarian, and work together with the student.
>
> We do not work with a computer—to find information we use a cardex or the librarian locates the needed subjects. Since our library only has 4,000 volumes it is easy to locate materials. . . . Libraries throughout Chile have only recently begun implementing Internet computer services. In our case we do not have the sophisticated equipment but I can tell you that some schools do have computer labs and are connected to the Internet. (Escobar Mamani 1998, my translation)

Puerto Rico

In Puerto Rico, libraries have a tradition of children's services, but there are few services to young adults. As with libraries in other Latin American countries, those in Puerto Rico lack adequate administrative, budget, and personnel support as well as the equipment and materials necessary to expand services to the young adult population. The services that librarians see as most important to patrons include reference, patron assistance, programs on topics of interest, arts and crafts workshops, and cultural programming.

Of the 141 public libraries on the island, which is similar in size and population to the state of Connecticut, 127 are under the direction of the Department of Education, 9 are municipal libraries with employees appointed by the mayor, and 5 are community libraries run by local boards. From the sampling of libraries surveyed by Milagros Otero Guzmán (1999), it was found that only one librarian (6 percent) had a master of library science (MLS) degree, while eight or 50 percent had bachelor's degrees, including some in the area of elementary education, and the rest had associate in arts degree or no degree. It has been suggested that libraries under the Department of Education could better serve the public if they were moved to the jurisdiction of municipalities, where they could seek support from local people, businesses, and agencies. This had indeed begun to happen. The majority of Puerto Rican public libraries are open from 8 AM to 4:30 PM, Monday through Friday, with very few open on Saturdays or evenings, and even fewer open on Sundays.

Although most of the Puerto Ricans many of us will encounter have probably lived in the United States for some time, a perspective on library services in that territory can be helpful, especially as we consider the lack of a library tradition among them.

■ In Closing

Whether from North, Central, or South America, we are all Americans—something those of us from the United States tend to overlook. As pointed out by Fernández-Shaw in *The Hispanic Presence in North America from 1492 to Today* (1987), nearly every state of the Union has place-names influenced by the Spanish. The Spanish influence in the Western Hemisphere dates from the 1500s and undoubtedly will continue, so we need to discover ways to blend the strengths of the Hispanic and Anglo cultures (as well as others) to best meet the needs of our increasingly diverse society. If we can get past feeling threatened by these developments, it can be a great adventure.

■ Works Cited

Acuña, Rodolfo. *Occupied America: A History of Chicanos*. New York: HarperCollins, 1988.

Almonte E., Ernesto. Personal communication. 30 June 1998.

Carrasquillo, Angela L. *Hispanic Children and Youth in the United States: A Resource Guide*. New York: Garland, 1991.

Chickering, Sharon K. "One Tough Road," *Colorado Central* (February 1997): 14–19.

Cuello, José. *Latinos and Hispanics: A Primer on Terminology.* (1996). [Online]. Available: http://clnet.ucr.edu/library/reforma/refogold.htm#Why (Accessed Dec. 19, 1997).

Escobar Mamani, Maritza Elsa. Personal communication. September 1998

"Facts on Hispanics," *The Voice of Hispanic Higher Education* (February 1998): 8.

Fernández-Shaw, Carlos M. *The Hispanic Presence in North America from 1492 to Today*. New York: Facts on File, 1987.

Gann, L. H. and Peter J. Duignan. *The Hispanics in the United States: A History*. Boulder, Colo.: Westview Press, 1986.

Hispanic Business (March 1998): 16.

Latin American Research and Service Agency. *LARASA/Report: A Publication About Latinos in Colorado.* (Jan.1995; March, May 1997; April 1998).

Martinez, Rosalie. Personal interview. 18 May 1998.

McWilliams, Carey. *North from Mexico: The Spanish-Speaking People of the United States.* New York: Greenwood Press, 1990.

Mendosa, Rick. "What's Up With Teenagers?" *Hispanic Business* (July–August 1998): 58–62.

Mestre, Lori S. and Sonia Nieto. "Puerto Rican Children's Literature and Culture in the Public Library," *MultiCultural Review* (June 1996): 26–39.

Otero Guzmán, Milagros. "Library Services to the Youth in Puerto Rican Public Libraries." Paper presented at the Trejo Foster Foundation Hispanic Library Education Institute in Tampa, FL, March 1999. In: *Library Services to Youth of Hispanic Heritage*, edited by Barbara Immroth and Kathleen de la Peña McCook. Jefferson, N.C.: McFarland, 2000.

Our Nation on the Fault Line: Hispanic American Education, September 1996. (1996) [Online] Available: http://www.ed.gov/pubs/FaultLine/call.html (Accessed April 2, 1998).

Romberg, Raquel. "Saints in the Barrio: Shifting, Hybrid, and Bicultural Practices in a Puerto Rican Community," *MultiCultural Review* (June 1996): 16–23.

Shorris, Earl. *Latinos: A Biography of the People.* New York: W. W. Norton, 1992.

U.S. Bureau of the Census. *The Hispanic Population in the United States: Population Characteristics.* Feb. 200. [On-line] Available: http:www.census.gov/prod/2000pubs/p20-527.pdf

———*Resident Population of the United States: Estimates, by Sex, Race, and Hispanic origin, with Median Age.* 30 April 1998. [Online] Available: http://www.census.gov/population/estimates/nation/intfile3-1.txt (Accessed May 16, 1998).

———*Statistical Abstract of the United States: 1997* (117th edition.) Washington, D.C., 1997.

Uquillas, Guadalupe. Personal communication. 28 April 1998.

White, Cherie R. Personal communication. 5 May 1998.

Chapter 2

Adult Services

■ Where to Begin?

The challenges of serving patrons with limited English skills are nothing new for U.S. librarians, but many of us may have assumed that it was a problem for the larger libraries to tackle—Los Angeles, New York, Miami. We in smaller communities did not have much to worry about as we could just depend on interlibrary loan for the few foreign-language requests we did receive. Suddenly (or so it seems) things have changed.

Community needs assessments are standard practice to analyze library clientele, and Alire and Archibeque detailed the process in *Serving Latino Communities* (66–94, 178–180). But what happens when the Spanish speakers arrive just after the 10-year census has been completed and you cannot wait eight or even four more years to begin finding out about them? Network with other professionals.

The school district librarian may be one of the first to notice the trend when the number of monolingual Spanish-speaking children enrolling in the schools begins increasing rapidly from one year to the next or even in the middle of the year. The city or county's public health nurse could document the number of Spanish-speakers who are bringing children for low-cost immunization clinics and related services, and additional information can be found by consulting with the Department of Social Services and local clergy. Furthermore, as you go about your daily routines, listen for other languages being spoken in supermarket aisles, discount stores, and self-service laundries or even among service personnel in the hallways of hotels where nearby library conventions are held.

With any brand-new population, it is difficult to know where to begin. Do you go in blind and try to survey them about their needs, or do you buy materials first and hope you guess right? A combination of these two techniques works in the early stages. In our case, the school librarian had the best idea of her curriculum-related needs, and we public and community college librarians rode along on her coattails. We began slowly and sought the advice of long-time Latino residents and teachers in our community as well as a nearby vendor. Other librarians in your state who have already successfully dealt with some of these issues could also offer valuable assistance.

We made some mistakes in our initial purchases, but at least had some material to offer Spanish-speakers who ventured in our doors as well as a reason to encourage ESL instructors to bring their classes to the library on field trips. In addition, having the material was an extra incentive to work at outreach services where it would be used so we could attract more patrons with whom we could begin to connect to better ascertain their real needs.

Although many librarians have found the best way to entice adults into the library is through their children, the Adult Services chapter had our primary focus because without the adults, the children would not be in our communities. Many of the ideas presented could apply to a variety of library types, so we hope you will take the ideas and change and shape them to meet your unique situations.

■ Making Connections

A study reported by Lynch in *American Libraries* (1997) showed that "households headed by a Hispanic person are least likely" to use a public library. In a personal conversation (Sept. 1998), author Pat Mora explained why this might be so. She said that besides the fact that free library service for people of all socioeconomic levels is not a strong tradition in Latin America, Latinos, in many subtle ways, have not been made welcome in our libraries and therefore have learned not to come to such places. In addition, immigrants may feel they do not deserve respect and may feel uncomfortable with the amount of time we librarians and other community workers are willing to spend with them because they have little money or low social status. Their lower status in the community is constantly reinforced, even if unintentionally.

A friendly greeting in one's first language, along with a smile and eye contact work wonders to help break down potential barriers and make patrons feel comfortable. One of the most important factors that librarians mention over and over for attracting Spanish-speaking patrons is having staff who speak the language. Even I, an experienced library user, look for a sympathetic, understanding face when I venture into a new library. How much more important that would be for a potential new patron who may have little or no previous library experience.

The ideal would be to have a staff person(s) of the same national origin(s) as the targeted population(s), but barring that, any Spanish-speakers are an asset as long as they are open-minded and try to minimize any personal biases. It has been my experience that if one makes an honest effort to speak Spanish and to understand the response, native speakers are quite forgiving of mistakes. Spanish-speaking staff at the Denver Public Library have *Hablo Español* printed at the bottom of their nametags for easy identification.

Although volunteers are often important members of a library's service team, it may be difficult to secure any from the targeted population because it is becoming increasingly necessary for more than one family member to be employed to make ends meet, especially if they have relatively low-paying jobs. Other sources of volunteers to help serve Spanish-speakers could be Americorps or Vista workers, native Spanish-speaking students, returned Peace Corps volunteers, teachers, college and high school students enrolled in Spanish, grandparents or other relatives of Spanish-speakers, and any other community member who speaks the language. A long-term goal of every library should be the identifying and mentoring (however informal) of possible future employees so that as part- and full-time positions become available, Spanish-speaking staff can be added. Encouraging staff members to take Spanish classes at the local community college is a good step; even better if you can help with the cost of tuition and books, and/or give released time to attend the classes.

Sensitivity Training

Although the library's governing board has been supportive since the beginning of outreach programming to Spanish-speakers, it is important to provide cultural awareness training to everyone associated with the library—from the board down to the custodians and volunteers. Potential patrons will keep coming to the library or be deterred depending on the people they meet and how they are made to feel. Even an inadvertent remark or unfortunate body language could offend someone. I can personally think of business establishments I have stopped frequenting because I was not treated as a valued customer—the clerks acting as if they could not be bothered waiting on me. That is not the feeling we want our patrons to receive.

We librarians do not have all the answers to the needs of our Spanish-speaking patrons, but our zeal to help may seem patronizing. This could be a problem if library volunteers or paid staff were native Spanish-speakers of an upper socioeconomic level. Their attempts to help working-class Spanish-speakers might be seen as self-serving attempts to preserve the status quo.

It may take some time for newly arrived Spanish-speakers to become comfortable using the library and begin defining and then articulating for themselves the services libraries could offer them. As a Hispanic library staff person in Denver told me: "Most of us were not raised with libraries." Patience is cautioned as we wait for relationships to be established and for leaders to emerge from that population with whom we can work. We may be the ones placed in the role of learners as we seek to understand a new (to us) culture and learn to empower these different people by taking them seriously, on their terms, not just on ours.

When I lived in Chile I found that some people automatically assumed I was of higher social status because I was a college graduate. To break down that barrier I worked to find areas in which they knew more than I and in which I could learn from them—areas such as cooking traditional dishes, handicrafts, gardening techniques, child-care tips, and always, the Spanish language. By creating more egalitarian relationships, my Chilean friends and I were helping each other reciprocally and I learned to deal with situations using their standards, not my engrained ones from the United States. No one of us did all the giving or all the receiving.

As our U.S. society practices less and less formality, we need to recognize that not all people feel at ease having others address them by first name unless they are well acquainted otherwise. Because Latinos are accustomed to using titles more than many of us may be, we can show respect by addressing a married or older women as *Señora*, an unmarried or younger one as *Señorita*, and man as *Señor*.

It is critical to Spanish-speakers' comfort levels to avoid embarrassing situations in the library. Adults and older students may be very shy about trying to speak in English, and it could take some time for them to get over that hesitancy. If a staff person cannot understand the patron's request, the staff should apologize and make it his or her fault, and not that of the patron. It would therefore be my fault that I don't understand Spanish or fractured English as well as I should, not the patron's fault that the patron does not speak better English. Sometimes humor at one's own expense will help ease the situation.

In the Door

The first introduction many adult patrons have to the library is by accompanying their children who are already familiar with the school or public library through school classes. We hope to make a good impression so they will feel welcome to return to seek information for their own benefit.

I am impressed when I telephone libraries and have a choice of hearing recorded information in either English or Spanish. Even a brief greeting in Spanish could make a difference. Signage should be bilingual so patrons can find their own way as much as possible, or at least feel a little less intimidated in this new setting. The Spanish vocabulary list in Appendix B should help with the signage, but if you have to go beyond the library staff for translations, do not overburden one person (such as the high school Spanish teacher) especially if you are counting on that person to volunteer his or her services. If you cannot afford to pay for the translation(s), arrange a mutually beneficial trade of services. It is also wise to have a second person check any translations because people who are not as fluent as they think they are sometimes volunteer for such tasks. Computer translations are risky because the literal interpretations can often be almost unintelligible or even offensive.

Place the library's Spanish-language material in a pleasant, readily visible space, not in a back corner where it must be sought out. The same is true of low-level, high-interest materials suitable for adults just learning English. In that light, adults should also be given easy access to children's materials, and not be embarrassed or discouraged from using them. I like to encourage adults to check out bilingual children's stories because they can read to their children in Spanish, but practice their English skills with the same book.

Most online computer catalogs do not have a foreign-language interface and may be "insurmountable obstacles" for non-English speakers (Castro 1990, 44). Online catalogs will be discussed in more detail in Chapter 6, but because of potential difficulties in use, you may want to make the collection easy to browse. Castro also suggests that a vertical file of clippings (with bilingual subject headings) be maintained for periodicals without indexing.

When Linda Payne-Button (1998) worked at the San Antonio Public Library, she developed a manual for Service Desk personnel listing all services offered in Spanish including relevant classes such as English as a Second Language (ESL), GED (General Equivalency Degree), and citizenship that were offered at various branches; suggested sources for Hispanic statistics in government documents; procured translations of common library questions; and provided lists of other library branches offering Spanish-language materials and maps showing physical locations of those branches, Spanish-language periodicals, and bilingual staff. She also included addresses and phone numbers for other community agencies providing services to immigrants. A brochure adverting these services could be distributed in the community. All library forms in San Antonio are available in Spanish including interlibrary loan requests, reconsideration of library materials forms, and suggested purchases, as well as the docents tour of the new library building.

If at all possible, the reference librarian should speak Spanish so adults do not have to depend on children to "broker" or mediate communication for them on such sensitive issues as birth control, spousal abuse, or health issues (McQuillan and Tse 1995, 195). Having patrons write down their question(s) might make the questions easier to understand (eliminating the accent or unclear speech variable) and/or allow the librarian to consult with another Spanish-speaker and contact the patron later with the answer (Milo 1990, 29). Forms printed in Spanish with an explanation of this technique, along with a promise of confidentiality, could aid the process and keep children out of the loop. An example of such a form can be found in *Latino Librarianship*, edited by Güereña (147).

■ Materials Selection

Whenever the topic of selecting Spanish-language materials arises, there is a question of the preferred origin of these materials. Can Mexican children understand Spanish from books written in Spain; can children from the Dominican Republic be expected to read books written in Argentina? The conclusion I reached after consulting with a number of people is that well-written Spanish from any Spanish-speaking country can be understood by Spanish-speakers worldwide. There are differences in vocabulary and idiomatic expressions, but in context they are usually readily understandable, or can be deciphered with the help of a dictionary. If it is a choice of monolingual Spanish-speakers trying to gain information from a book in English versus one in Spanish from a "foreign" country, the latter is much preferable.

We in the United States do not avoid Dickens, Shakespeare, or Chaucer because they were written in British English. And, we are encouraged to read works by Dante, Cervantes, and Dostoyevsky even though most of us probably read them in translation, not the original text. In addition, because the publishing industry is not as highly developed in Latin America and Spain as it is in Great Britain and the United States, a library wishing to acquire a book on a particular topic may not have a choice of publishers.

A rule of thumb is to select material in this order, as available:

1. Written or translated by a native speaker of the country of origin of local Spanish-speaking residents. Because more Latinos in the United States are from Mexico, the majority of libraries would prefer Mexican Spanish. One negative factor is that the physical quality of books published in Latin American countries tends to be inferior to those published in the United States.

2. Written or translated by a native speaker of another Latin American country

3. Written or translated in Spain

4. Translated into Spanish in the United States

An encouraging sign is that more Spanish-language books are being published in the United States, some publishers even releasing simultaneous editions in English and Spanish. The decision as to which titles to release this way, however, may be based on purely economic factors (i.e., which titles offer potential for the highest distribution and most profit), not on literary merit. Another concern is that capable translators complete translations. When translated poorly, these texts do not read with the natural cadence and flow of Spanish and can have misspellings, and grammatical and contextual errors (Schon 1995, 318–319).

Availability of Titles

The availability of Spanish-language editions is further complicated by the fact that an English-language publisher may sell translation and distribution rights for some of its titles to one publisher and for different titles to another. In a personal letter dated 16 April 1998, the Dorling Kindersley (DK) Adult Sales Manager for Spain explained that DK does not publish books in Spanish but does license books to Spanish and Latin American publishers who translate and publish the books for their respective markets. DK's titles have been sold to several different publishers in various countries. Therefore, the books one sees for sale during a trip to Mexico or Ecuador may not be available for purchase in the United States if that particular Spanish-language publisher does not have distribution rights in this country.

Articles in *Publishers Weekly* detail trends in publishing in Latin America as well as the rest of the world. Consulting this magazine would help you keep up with what is happening in the Spanish-language book trade. You would therefore know which publishers are publishing the best Spanish-language material at the moment, what is available for purchase, which publishers have begun to improve on the physical and aesthetic qualities of these books, and the age levels for which they publish. The articles can also be accessed online at: http://www.publishersweekly.com.

When I visited a large bookstore in San José, Costa Rica, and asked who the most popular author was for women, I was directed to shelves with books written by Danielle Steele. Even though Spanish-speakers want to read the same popular books as English-speakers, libraries should try to have a good selection of culturally relevant materials by Latino authors. Unfortunately, Latinos have learned from us that everything from North America is to be valued and items from their countries are inferior. While providing people with materials they want to read, we should also give them the opportunity to appreciate the creative, positive aspects of their own cultural heritage—values from which we *norteños* (northerners) can also learn because no one culture has a monopoly on good ideas.

Popular Adult Topics

Although you must get to know your Spanish-speaking patrons to determine what resources they really want and need, the following is a list of subject areas that librarians have mentioned as being popular with Spanish-speaking adults (Adelante 1994; Shapiro 1997):

• Alcoholism	• Health & beauty, exercise & fitness
• Astrology and the occult	• High-low books in English
• Auto repair	• History & government of United
• Bilingual books	States and Mexico
• Biographies: U.S. presidents, Latino role models	• Home repair
• Business and careers	• How-to
• Citizenship	• Legal rights & responsibilities
• Computer basics, Internet	• Literacy materials: English and/or Spanish
• Consumer issues such as time payments, interest rates, avoiding debt	• Motivation, Self-esteem
• Cooking	• New Age
• Dictionaries, encyclopedias, almanacs	• Newspapers from population's place of origin
• English as a second language (all formats)	• Parenting and child care
• Fiction	• Physician's Desk Reference
• Fotonovelas (adult-type comic books)	• Pop culture
• Government publications in Spanish	• Sewing
• Green card, how to secure	• Sex education, pregnancy, and childbirth
	• Survival skills

If at all possible, try to examine Spanish-language books before purchasing them. If several libraries come together in one setting, vendors may be willing to bring books to you for examination as was done in Bridgeport, Conn., where book fairs were organized to benefit the development of area Spanish-language collections (Everett 1998). This arrangement would also assist with cooperative collection development, as librarians could discuss at the book fair who would purchase what type of material and thus avoid unnecessary duplication.

Unless you know in advance that you have an especially well-educated, literate clientele, I would not invest heavily in literature classics, but in the beginning would concentrate on popular fiction and practical nonfiction. You can always add the classics to the collection later as demand warrants. However, an excellent booklet for use in identifying significant historic and contemporary Hispanic authors is *Latin American Literature Pathfinder*, available from REFORMA de Utah (P. O. Box 521271, Salt Lake City, UT 84152-1271).

Physical Quality

You may have to lower some of your standards on physical quality as well as collect more ephemeral materials in order to provide as much selection of reading materials as possible. Once you begin collecting Spanish-language materials, these materials need to be a regular part of the buying cycle, even if you are as lucky as we in receiving a Library Services and Construction Act (LSCA), now the Library Services and Technology Act (LSTA) grant to begin your initial collection. You want your Spanish-speaking patrons to know you are serious about meeting their needs with attractive materials in good repair, not just buying materials when you have a little extra money. Grant monies can provide a nice infusion of dollars and boost the staff's morale, but cannot be the sole source of funds if you are serious about serving this population. A chapter in Alire and Archibeque's *Serving Latino Communities* (121–140) details steps to writing successful grant proposals.

Collaboration

Although time consuming, it may pay to look beyond traditional library funding sources to other agencies that sponsor projects dealing with such issues as women's and children's health, youth and substance abuse prevention, and employment assistance. Many of us are in one-professional libraries, but it is not such a lonely venture if we can work cooperatively with other community agencies to secure funding and then implement the resulting program(s). The collaborating agency could, for instance, offer grant-funded workshops or classes, perhaps in the library's community meeting room, and then encourage patrons to visit the library's Spanish-language collection to borrow additional materials that have been purchased to support the program.

■ Promoting the Library

Outreach to people who do not have a tradition of library use will take effort and creativity. Latinos have the same basic informational needs as everyone but they often develop other avenues to have those needs met—likely through networking with family and friends. Libraries therefore must reach out, not wait for people to come to them.

Getting the Word Out

As mentioned earlier, adults are often motivated to come to the school or public library when their children are required to do class assignments. If library staff make the adults feel comfortable and welcome when they first arrive, and also take time to show them the range of materials available for them as well as their students, they are more likely to return at a future date. An article in the Hobbs, New Mexico *News-Sun* (Morgan 1994), tells the story of a young Latina mother who ventured into the Lovington Public Library for the first time when her seven-year-old daughter had a school assignment to complete. Because the mother and daughter found friendly, Spanish-speaking staff, and the Spanish-language materials they needed, the visit was a success for all involved.

The library should create a high profile in the community. Word-of-mouth advertising is as critical as are personal invitations to the library and its programs. Public service announcements (in Spanish) on local radio and television stations can also be effective. Lower-income Latinos are not accustomed to reading anything, so written notices and flyers may not attract their attention. Nevertheless, Spanish-language posters and fliers could be distributed to places where people congregate: grocery stores, self-service laundries, restaurants, churches, neighborhood centers, apartment buildings, hair salons, video rental stores, day-care centers, bus stops, Social Service offices, and health departments. If your city allows advertisements on the sides of its buses, how about trying to get some bilingual advertising for the library?

Staff also need to assess how the library's physical location affects usage. If the building is not in a highly visible location, steps need to be taken to overcome that liability, perhaps by taking library services out into the community. Get the Hispanic Chamber of Commerce to assist in outreach and promotion. Other examples of outreach will be noted later in this chapter.

Colorado Mountain College, which runs the local public access television station in Leadville, arranged to videotape a Mexican family (recruited by the bilingual aide at the elementary school) as they used local libraries. The five family members had no speaking parts, but voice-overs in English and Spanish provided information about the libraries' hours and services. The family and all their friends were delighted to see them as television stars. Librarians can arrange for the local Spanish-language newspaper to carry library hours, and to write periodic articles featuring the library. If you have staff or volunteers who can write and submit interesting articles, the Spanish-language newspaper (especially if it has limited staff) may be more willing to run them.

Out into the Community

Many libraries take advantage of health fairs, celebrations, festivals, and literacy fairs to take library card sign-up booths into the community, and to emphasize that services are free. While you are out at the community event, visit booths of other organizations to look for ideas for future programs.

In Houston, library staff marched in the Little League parade at the beginning of baseball season and set up a library registration table alongside the Little League registration. Other possibilities include handing out applications at schools' parent-teacher conferences, at ESL or GED classes, or during coffee hour at church. If all the necessary information is filled in on the application, it could be entered into the library computer later. Although you may need some verification of a person's address, try to refrain from asking for an identification (ID) because that may imply the potential Spanish-speaking patrons need to have an official status in this country or that the library is part of the governmental establishment checking up on them.

When possible, hand the future patron a temporary library card on the spot. My experience has been that having a library card in hand may act as an admission ticket—one less hurdle to overcome for the Spanish-speaking patron who wishes to enter the library.

Martín Rivera (1998) of the Tucson-Pima Public Library (Ariz.) says that in situations where he is not sure in which language people are most comfortable, he speaks in a bilingual format. He thus gives people an indication that he can speak in either language, and they can follow up with questions in the language they prefer. While he's at it, he could hand out bilingual refrigerator magnets or bookmarks with library hours and services, or coupons for a free book on the patron's first visit to the library.

Marketing

Roslow and Nicholls in a *Journal of Advertising Research* (1996) article showed that Spanish-language advertising on television more positively influences Hispanics. Many libraries provide bilingual advertising in an attempt to reach two markets at once, but as Alma Flor Ada pointed out, Spanish-speakers may perceive that they are being served as an afterthought, as second-class citizens. An added dilemma is that if libraries do provide effective advertising in Spanish, patrons will expect service in Spanish, increasing the need for staff who are fluent or can get by, in that language. Before doing any advertising, analyze the purpose of the service or program. You may find that bilingual advertising could serve the purpose, or that parallel signs or public service announcements, some in English and some in Spanish, should be placed in various locations around town.

Examining issues of *Hispanic Business* will uncover examples of effective marketing strategies. To complement values often held by Latinos, the advertising should be aimed at intergenerational families, reflect wholesome family values, engender trust or loyalty, and demonstrate admiration and respect. Although commercial marketing appeals to parents' desires to buy the best for their children, library marketing should emphasize how families, with little or no outlay of funds, together with libraries, can give children the best gift there is—the gift of literacy (Mora 1998).

Now, if libraries could just create mascots as appealing as Taco Bell's Chihuahua, Dinky, we'd have patrons flocking in our doors.

■ Outreach Programming

Librarians have many great programming ideas, but needless to say, not all ideas will work in every community. A program that really takes off in one community, may fall flat in another. Often it is a matter of finding the right time, meeting place, and staff person to ensure success. People who have not had positive educational experiences may not feel at ease coming to a schoolroom for a workshop or class. Is there another location in the community where they would feel more at ease? A church or community center, or the public library instead of the school library, for instance?

Other factors to be considered include: which days of the week and hours of the day are most convenient (if you are in a resort area as I am, people may have free days in the middle of the week, and not on weekends); will transportation be a problem; does poor weather restrict travel in the winter; will child care be necessary; will family members be returning to the home country at certain times of the year and/or do they relocate periodically?

Maria DeHerrera (1998) of Conejos County, Colorado, says she sponsors programs that people need, whether about pregnancy or how to dress an elk. She also suggests programs that get people involved, such as making tamales. It is often hard to determine which programs patrons can best use to improve the quality of their lives, but the key is getting to know the people and establishing rapport. Library staff need not lead every event, but can offer the facilities to other agencies and individuals willing to do the actual programs. Once you can find leaders of the targeted community to offer programs, you will probably have a ready-made audience, even if it consists mainly of aunts, uncles, cousins, and in-laws.

As a turnabout, encourage Spanish-speakers to lead sessions on popular skills like cooking, arts and crafts, or Spanish conversation for the non-Latino community. Or, contact your state's Cooperative Extension Service for some programs and/or free pamphlets in Spanish.

English and Literacy

Materials on learning English are more likely to be in high demand in libraries serving LEP patrons. Offering ESL classes at the library or collaborating with other agencies who do offer the classes can help introduce immigrants to library services. If the classes are not actually held in the library, make sure bilingual or easy English-language books are taken to class for Spanish-speaking student perusal, and that those students are given tours of the facility. Variations of the ESL program can include encouraging the reading of quality children's literature or books of the students' own choosing, and the showing of movies, followed by discussion (in English). One ESL teacher requested that the library purchase English-language films with Spanish subtitles. The Spanish-speaking students would be hearing the spoken English, but could keep up with the story line by reading the subtitles in their first language.

Intercambio at Colorado Mountain College (http://www.coloradomtn.edu) is a program to pair Latinos and Anglos in an informal setting to practice English and Spanish conversation skills. Each participant gets to be alternately student and teacher during the class period. There is also a component to meet the needs of any youngsters who accompany their parents.

In Michigan, libraries cooperating with nearby colleges recruited students to provide evening "Survival English" classes for seasonal migrant workers. These students were given training in how to work with the migrant workers and received academic credit for their efforts, so the program benefited everyone involved (Gilbert 1997).

On an even more basic level, some Latinos may need Adult Basic Education and literacy instruction in Spanish before tackling English.

General Education

Because many Mexican adults in the United States are lacking in basic education, the Mexican *Instituto Nacional para la Educación de los Adultos* (INEA) offers training and support to volunteer instructors in this country who will teach classes in literacy, and primary and secondary education for adults. Further information on the program can be secured from the nearest Mexican embassy.

GED classes may already be in place in the community through a local high school or college, but coordination with the public library can only strengthen the efforts. To supplement GED classes, Kentucky Educational Television (KET, The Kentucky Network, 600 Cooper Drive, Lexington, KY 40502-2296) offers a series of 44 half-hour lessons with unlimited duplication rights, in English and Spanish, for math, reading, and writing. Your local public television station may offer the series, and testing opportunities may be available in your area, or the videos could be used to supplement another GED program.

Life Skills

The Fresno County (Calif.) Free Library has offered programs on legal and consumer issues with the help of a grant from the Bank of America (a good example of looking beyond the usual library sources for funds). Ideas from the Queens Borough Public Library include workshops on immigration law, workers' and tenants' rights, and the American educational system—all areas in which an immigrant's previous experience may differ significantly from what they encounter in this country (Chao 1993). An additional idea might be a program on managing credit card debt.

Migrant workers especially need information on such topics as child care, pre- and neonatal care, and legal and social services rights. Librarians working with migrants in Florida found that free programs that they offered on pesticide training were not well attended because supervisors had (erroneously) told the workers that there was a charge to attend. Migrant workers may not realize that the government does provide some free services and that they have a right to take advantage of them (Abramoff and Cors 1999).

Conejos County Library received a State of Colorado Initiative Grant to offer training for parents and day-care workers on how to effectively read to children (DeHerrera 1998). Other libraries have offered programs to train day-care workers or to allow women to obtain home child-care licensing—jobs that might appeal to those who need extra income but do not wish to leave their own preschoolers in the care of others. Public and school libraries could offer collections of materials on parenting skills for adults, as well as books and recordings that could be used with day-care children.

Job Search Clubs, perhaps in conjunction with the local unemployment office, could offer training in finding employment, completing application forms, writing resumes, interviewing skills, and learning basic employer expectations for the Spanish-speaking patrons in your community.

Or how about a free workshop given by qualified tax advisors on how to complete income tax forms? Houston Public Library has teamed with a local college with an accounting program to have students, who need field work experience as part of their degree, come to the library to give tax advice. The assistance is given every Saturday from the beginning of February until April 15 and was so popular that in 1999 they hardly had to advertise. At the beginning of the program, library staff translated for the accounting students, but now the accounting students all speak Spanish themselves (Morales 1999). Maria DeHerrera (1998) has found patrons also need help with other kinds of forms such as LEAP (Low Income Energy Assistance Program), and she includes notices of related programs with checks distributed through the Department of Social Services.

Not all libraries have had success offering computer classes for Spanish-speaking patrons, but the Public Library of Charlotte and Mecklenberg County (N.C.), which offers a series of four two-hour Saturday morning or afternoon sessions, has a waiting list of people wanting to take the class. Ten people in each class receive instruction on Computer Basics for Beginners, Microsoft® Word Concepts I and II, and Introduction to the Internet. Each participant who completes the program receives a diploma at the end of the series of classes. Once people finish the classes they want to return the favor, so they act as assistants to the instructor. In this way the library is developing a network of volunteers whose talents can be tapped (Patterson 1999).

Citizenship classes are offered at the San Diego Public Library on Saturdays: in English in the mornings and in Spanish in the afternoons. The library has been partnering with an adult school for about two years so they avoid unnecessary duplication of efforts (Gonzalez 1998).

Bookmobile (Bibliobús)

The library bookmobile as a way to reach isolated families is not a new idea, but an interesting variation was developed by the Lake County Public Library in Leadville, Colorado To provide library services to stay-at-home women who lived in outlying trailer courts with no access to public transportation, the library arranged to rent a school bus with driver for a few hours one morning a week. A bilingual Mexican native was hired to coordinate the new service and during the first run library staff went door-to-door with bilingual fliers. A banner taped to the bus advertised the service. It was difficult to determine the best day of the week to offer the service because survey results showed a wide discrepancy in convenient times. Materials for the bookmobile came from the collections of the public and community college libraries. Although the service was deemed successful, no funds were forthcoming for the public library to continue it for another year.

Instead, The Center, a nationally recognized child-care center in Leadville, was able to secure Youth Crime Prevention Intervention grant funding from the state and picked up the bookmobile service as part of the duties of its Family Literacy Coordinator. Transportation is now provided by a Head Start bus, and the public library still lends a portion of the materials.

The Center uses the bookmobile to communicate with families and find out how things are going in addition to encouraging families in reading activities. The coordinator attempts to make the experience nonthreatening, by serving coffee and donuts as people browse. An evaluative comment made by a participant at the end of the first year gave one of the best reasons for continuing the service: "We need somebody to understand us."

Another idea would be for the bookmobile to schedule stops at schools to conveniently coincide with the end of the day when parents arrive to pick up their children. With support from the school staff, children could encourage and assist their parents in using the bookmobile.

Deposit Collections

Unexpected challenges can be seen from the Lake County (Colo.) Public Library's experience with deposit collections as reported in its project outline and evaluation:

> Seed collections (i.e., Swap-a-Book) of 150 Spanish, English, and bilingual adult and pre-school books were placed in three non-profit agencies during the project year.
>
> a. A collection of new, inexpensive Spanish-language paperbacks was purchased.
>
> b. A Spanish-language bookplate was created and placed in each book, indicating participation locations and phone numbers. A second bookplate was added that says in Spanish: Welcome to the library. Please return this book to any one of the community libraries.
>
> c. The books were distributed in plastic crates to a Catholic church, public health office, and community day care center.
>
> d. The health office felt the books would get more use in the WIC (Women, Children, and Infants) office, so moved them there. However, the WIC staff found the books to be in the way when children scattered them over the floor, so at their request, we removed the crate to the public health lobby. Unfortunately here the crate got pushed behind a large planter where it was not readily visible.

e. At the day care center, the crate was first stored in an office, then retrieved and taken to an ESL classroom. The teacher there is doing an informal "check out" and those students are making good use of the books, but they aren't available to parents or the general public.

f. (Staff person) reports that the books are in a good location at the Catholic Church and are being well used there. (McCain 1996)

The project was implemented with the assumption that many of the books would disappear into the community and none of the cooperating agencies were being asked to account for them. Perhaps more groundwork needed to be done with agency personnel (and not just the director) to help them feel a sense of ownership and partnership in the project.

Cultural/Enrichment Events

Cultural/enrichment programming can be fun for everyone—Latinos as well as the rest of us who are learning to appreciate the richness of other cultures. According to Margarita Ortiz (1998) of the Bowen Branch of the Detroit Public Library, the most successful programs they have sponsored over the last 20 or so years have appealed to the ethnicity of the community. The library plans activities with other cultural groups to "inspire and promote the love of Latino-Hispanic culture." Some of the early programs involved showing films from Hispanic countries.

For Valentine's Day, the Houston Public Library held four highly successful Saturday programs of Spanish-oriented romantic poetry and music. While adults listened to the poetry reading by guest poets and local celebrities, children participated in a crafts program. Between readings, a local trio of musicians played soft music. Some mothers opted to stay with their youngsters in the children's program, instead of listening to the readings, but that was all right. One of the programs was done bilingually, with the others in Spanish. A local company donated the snacks.

Local musicians, dancers, actors, or singers may be willing to appear at special programs or celebrations free of charge or for a modest fee. Houston Public Library paid its musicians, and the musicians were so popular the library plans to have them again (Morales 1999). The Ft. Lupton (Colo.) Library, a combined public/school library, has had an all-district art show to showcase student work. Spanish-speaking parents were given a special tour of the exhibit with appropriate explanations.

Discover the special holidays for the population in your area and use these holidays as occasions for special displays and/or programming, not just for the benefit of Latinos, but as cultural awareness opportunities for non-Latinos as well. Some popular holidays are: Hispanic Heritage Month from mid-September to mid-October, *Cinco de Mayo* (May 5) celebrating the Mexican Army's Victory over the French in 1862, and on November 2 *Día de los Muertos* when families pay honor to their dead loved ones. You could also have fun with April 23 that is celebrated in Barcelona, Spain, as Book Day and Lover's Day. Book and flower stands are set up around the city; men give women roses while women return the favor with the gift of a book. In addition, William Shakespeare and Miguel de Cervantes died April 23 in 1616.

The Tucumcari (New Mexico) Public Library finds that its extensive video collection encourages patron visits. Once patrons are accustomed to borrowing videos, they often branch out into other material (Rey 1998).

In one community with no Spanish-language cable television service, the local college connects with a Mexico City television station via satellite and broadcasts programs on weekends over the educational access channel when there is no regular programming scheduled.

■ Periodicals

The main criterion for selection of periodical titles for this section was that they be available for a direct subscription from a U.S. address or through a U.S. distributor. In the latter case they might be mailed from another country, but the distributor would handle the paperwork and any problems. In addition, I previewed most of the titles personally. A number of quality Spanish-language periodicals are available worldwide, but obtaining them can be frustrating. Some of the titles listed in this list would be appropriate for teens, and some of the titles listed in Chapter 5 would be appropriate for adults.

One suggestion, especially for libraries with limited periodical budgets, is to work with a local bookstore and arrange to purchase outdated Spanish-language issues for a minimal fee—perhaps for as little as a dime. Then, for the cost of a bar code plus the dime, you would have periodicals to add to the collection.

Of the periodical distribution companies responding to my inquiry for lists of Spanish-language titles they handle, EBSCO's was the most extensive, with many titles, not included here, that would be appropriate for specific industries or professions. In addition to this list, librarians can consult *Latino Periodicals* by Salvador Güereña and Vivian Pisano (McFarland, 1998).

Addresses of Distributors and Publishers

C.D.S., Subscriptions Dept.
PO Box 37253
Boone, IA 50037
http://www.cdsintl.com

Continental Book Company
625 E. 70th Ave. #5
Denver, CO 80229

Cooper Ave. #29
Glendale, NY 11385
http://www.continentalbook.com

EBSCO, International Headquarters
PO Box 11943
Birmingham, AL 35201-1943
http://www.ebsco.com/home/

Editorial América, S.A. (Grupo Televisa)
6355 N.W. 36th St.
Virginia Gardens, FL 33166 (Publisher)

Latin American Books Source, Inc.
48 Las Flores Dr.
Chula Vista, CA 91910

Latin American Periodicals
2555 N. Coyote Dr., Suite 109
Tucson, AZ 85745

Spanish Publications Inc.
PO Box 742149
Houston, TX 77274-2149

Spanish Periodicals & Book Sales
10100 NW 25th St.
Miami, FL 33172
http://www.spanishperiodical.com

Sun Periodical Corp.
PO Box 52423
Miami, FL 33152
http://www.spanishperiodical.com

Periodical Titles

Américas

Organization of American States (OAS)
19th Street and Constitution Avenue, NW
Washington, D.C. 20006

Subscription: PO Box 3000
Denville, NJ 07834-3000
or 1-800-222-5405; EBSCO

Describing itself as the "cultural arts magazine of the Hemisphere," this colorful, glossy bimonthly is published by the Organization of American States. Available in English and Spanish editions, articles feature various aspects of life in the 35 member nations of OAS. Each issue also has a column of book reviews, with occasional reviews of videos.

Artes de México

Distributed by: Latin American Books Source, Inc.;
EBSCO; Continental Book Co.

Glossy, artsy magazine with lots of colored photos with each issue devoted to a specific theme. English translations of articles provided at the back of each issue. Although a magazine, each issue could be cataloged separately and treated as a book.

Artistas: La revista de la juventud

Blue Ox Publishing Co., Inc.
Carr. #869, KM. 1.4, Bo.
Palmas, Cataño, PR 00962

Distributor: Spanish Periodicals

Self-proclaimed as the only youth magazine published in Puerto Rico, this small-sized biweekly primarily features articles on popular Latino artists.

Automóvil

Distributed by: C.D.S.; Continental Book Co.

A magazine about automobiles—always a popular subject with men and boys.

Box y Lucha

Distributed by: Latin American Periodicals; EBSCO

Magazine about boxing and wrestling.

Buenhogar: Edición en español de Good Housekeeping

Editorial América, S.A.; Distributors: EBSCO; Latin American Periodicals; Continental Book Co.; Subscription: C.D.S.

Like its English counterpart, although much slimmer, the monthly *Buenhogar* has articles on such topics as beauty, health, childrearing, marital relationships, home decoration, and fashion. Included also are the prerequisite sections of recipes and "My Problem and How I Solved It."

Cambio 16

Distributed by: EBSCO

Full-color, glossy, weekly news magazine from Spain, geared toward the more affluent. Sections deal with politics, economics, culture and society.

Casa & Estilo Internacional

Linda International Publishing, Inc.,
   Oficinas centrales de redacción y publicidad,
   12182 SW 128 St.
   Miami, FL 33186

Similar to *House Beautiful* or *Homes & Gardens*, this bimonthly is aimed at more affluent homes. English translations of articles are included.

Contenido

Distributed by: EBSCO; Latin American Periodicals

A monthly, little magazine from Mexico, with short articles on a variety of subjects.

Cosmopolitan en Español

Editorial América, S.A. Distributed by: EBSCO; Latin American Periodicals; Subscription: C.D.S.

Features the kinds of articles one would expect in *Cosmopolitan*: fashion and beauty, home and kitchen, relationships.

Cristina La Revista

Editorial América, S.A. Distributed by: Latin American Periodicals; EBSCO; Subscription: C.D.S

Although emphasizing Latinos of Hollywood fame, this monthly magazine, aimed at middle-class women, also has articles of substance, without the sensationalism of some other titles. In one issue examined, one could read about the mayor of Santo Domingo, Dominican Republic, and Dinky of Taco Bell. Other features include advice column, cooking, travel, and book reviews.

Diez Minutos

Distributed by: EBSCO; http://www.hachette.es

Subtitled "the heart of the news" this weekly magazine from Spain features news briefs about the lives of famous people.

Elle

> Editorial América, S.A.; Distributed by: EBSCO; Continental Book Co. Subscription: C.D.S.
>
> A monthly for the young woman interested in the latest in fashion (including top-name designers), beauty, male-female relationships and interior design. Also included are articles on health, recipes, and travel.

¡Entérese!

> Distributed by: Sun Periodical Corp.
>
> Although emphasizing interesting Latino personalities, articles in this monthly also cover events and people of world-wide interest such as U.S. movie stars, British Royal Family, and Russian Imperial Family. There seems to be less emphasis on scandal and sex than some of the other similar titles.

Epoca: Semanario de México

> Distributed by: Latin American Periodicals; EBSCO; Continental Book Co.
>
> A weekly news magazine like *Time* or *Newsweek*.

Estrellas

> Distributed by: Spanish Periodicals & Book Sales
>
> Appears to be similar to the tabloids, with all the latest "news" about entertainment stars.

Estylo: Latina Lifestyle

> 3660 Wilshire Blvd., Suite 714
> Los Angeles, CA 90010;
>
> Subscription: PO Box 16268
> North Hollywood, CA 91615-9988
>
> A bimonthly, bilingual, glossy magazine for stylish young Latinas with articles emphasizing health and beauty, fashion, and men. Although English is emphasized, all major articles are in both languages.

Fem: Publicación Feminista Mensual

> Distributed by EBSCO.
>
> A monthly feminist publication from Mexico.

Ganchillo Artístico
> Distributed by EBSCO.

>> A monthly crocheting magazine from Barcelona, Spain.

Glamour en Español
> Glamour en Español
> 1101 Brickell Ave., Piso 15
> Miami, FL 33131

>> A monthly magazine for more affluent young women with the majority of articles dealing with fashion, beauty, health, men, and sex.

Harper's Bazaar en Español
> Editorial América, S.A. Distributed by: EBSCO; Latin American Periodicals; Subscription: C.D.S

>> Covering the worlds of fashion, beauty, and culture, *Harper's Bazaar en Español* self-identifies itself as "the most avant-garde and diverse magazine of its type" (my translation).

Hispanic Business
> 360 S. Hope Ave., Suite 300C
> Santa Barbara, CA 93105
> www.hispanstar.com

>> Monthly except January/February and July/August and bimonthly in September and October. Although not a magazine for the Spanish-speaking, it provides a good resource on Hispanic marketing and trends of which librarians serving this population might like to be aware.

Hispanoamericano
> Distributed by: EBSCO.

>> A monthly news magazine from Mexico that appears more analytical than *Time* or *Newsweek*.

¡Hola!
> F.I.L. Inc.
> PO Box 164000-4000
> Miami, FL 33116.

> Distributed by: EBSCO; Continental Book Co.

>> A weekly magazine from Spain, this has the look of *Life* magazine, filled with color photos. Although European personalities

are featured, the issue examined also had spreads on such people as Barbara Streisand, Madonna, and Antonio Banderas.

Ideas Para Tu Hogar

Editorial América, S.A. Subscription: C.D.S. Distributed by: EBSCO; Latin American Periodicals

A full-color monthly similar to the U.S. version of *Good Housekeeping* with recipes, crafts, home decorating ideas, and gardening tips.

Impacto

Distributed by: EBSCO; Latin American Periodicals

A weekly news magazine with emphasis on events occurring in Mexico.

Kena Mensual

Distributed by: EBSCO; Latin American Periodicals

A monthly magazine for the fashionable young married/young mother concerned with health, beauty, home, and cuisine as well as the latest on the stars.

Latina: Magazine Bilingüe

Latina Publications
1500 Broadway
New York, NY 10036

Bilingual publication with articles on young Latina women, beauty, recipes, health, and men.

Macworld España

Distributed by: EBSCO

Spain's version of the computer magazine, *Macworld*.

Marie Claire: en Español

Editorial América, S.A. Distributed by: EBSCO; Continental Book Co.; Subscription: C.D.S.

Although this monthly woman's magazine has the usual articles on fashion, beauty, and cuisine, it also has some articles of substance on such topics as kidnapping of children, Viagra, suicide, and travel.

Men's Health, Hombre Saludable

Editorial América, S.A. Subscription: C.D.S. Distributed by: Latin American Periodicals

A monthly magazine for the young professional man concerned with health in its various aspects, and fitness.

MetaMundo Internacional

Distributed by: Spanish Periodicals & Book Sales

Articles dealing with the metaphysical or spiritual side of life.

Mi Gente: The English-Spanish Magazine for the Americas: La Revista en Español e Inglés Para las Américas

Gente Publishing Ltd.
5140 Dundas St. West, Suite 200
Toronto, Ontario, Canada M9A 1C2

Subscription: *Mi Gente* Magazine
PO Box 2804
Fargo, ND 58108-9891

A monthly, bilingual magazine dealing with economic conditions and politics in Latin America. The first issue included news on Venezuela, relations between Peru and Ecuador, and the Dominican Republic, along with the prerequisite sections on wines and cuisine.

Muy Interesante: La Revista Mensual Para Saber Más de Todo

Distributed by: EBSCO; Latin American Periodicals; Subscription: C.D.S.

A colorful, monthly science magazine for the layperson. Articles deal with such topics as astronomy, human body, health, behavior, and nature.

National Geographic en Español

Subscription: C.D.S.; Latin American Periodicals

With the familiar yellow-bordered cover photo, *National Geographic en Español* has the same quality articles as the English-language original. However, to appeal more specifically to Latino readers, two new sections have been added: Geographic Latin America and Conservation in Latin America.

Newsweek en Español

> Ideas & Capital,
> 1101 Brickell Ave., 15th Floor
> Miami, FL 33131
> Distributed by: Latin American Periodicals

> Slimmer than its English counterpart, the weekly issues do carry a few of the same articles that have been translated into Spanish. The magazine is distributed in 19 Latin American countries plus the United States.

PC Magazine en Español

> Editorial América, S.A.; Distributed by: EBSCO; Latin American Periodicals; Subscription: C.D.S.

> A slimmer version of the English magazine by the same title.

PC World

> IDG News Service, Latin American Bureau
> 5775 Blue Lagoon Dr., Suite 230
> Miami, FL 33126
> Distributed by: EBSCO.

> The major articles in this computer magazine are the same in the English and Spanish editions for same month, but the English edition is much larger.

Paula

> Distributed by: EBSCO

> A women's monthly from Mexico with the usual articles, but it also includes some articles about issues such as street children and an ecology crusade.

Proceso: Semanario de Información y Análisis

> Distributed by: EBSCO; Latin American Periodicals; Continental Book Co.

> As the title indicates, this is a weekly of current information and analysis from Mexico.

Salud Hoy

> Distributed by: Spanish Periodicals & Book Sales

> Deals with health issues of today's world.

Salud Total: El Médico en Su Hogar

Distributed by: Spanish Periodical & Book Sales

Black-and-white monthly with informative articles on topics dealing with common health problems or concerns.

Selecciones del Readers' Digest

Readers' Digest Latinoamérica, S.A.
2655 LeJeune Rd., Suite 301
Coral Gables, FL 33134-5823
Distributed by: EBSCO; Latin American Periodicals

The Spanish version of the familiar *Readers' Digest*, published monthly as is the English edition.

Ser Padres Hoy: Porque de tu Hijo se Trata

Distributed by: EBSCO

A monthly parenting magazine from Madrid, Spain with articles for moms and dads, although women would find the articles most helpful. The informative articles deal with pregnancy and children up to about age 10.

Siempre! Presencia en Mexico

Distributed by: EBSCO

A weekly news magazine from Mexico that is similar to *Time* or *Newsweek*.

TV y Novelas

Editorial América, S. A.; Distributors: Spanish Periodical & Books Sales, Inc., EBSCO; Subscription: C.D.S. Latin American Periodicals

For those (primarily women) who follow the soap operas (*telenovelas*) on Spanish-language television, and want to know the latest about their favorite television stars.

Van, Vanguardia en español

Egoiste Publications S.L.
302 Surfside Blvd.
Surfside, FL 33154

Published 10 times a year, this is an avant-garde magazine of fashion, cinema, and music.

Vanidades

Editorial América, S.A. Distributed by : EBSCO; Latin American Periodicals; Continental Book Co.; Subscription: C.D.S.

A biweekly for women with articles on fashion, beauty, and famous people.

Visión: La Revista Latinoamericana

Editorial Técnica S.A., (Section 889)
P. O. Box 02-5289
Miami, FL 33102; EBSCO

This biweekly publication is similar to *Business Week*, but with emphasis on Latin American countries.

Vogue Mexico

Distributed by: EBSCO

Vogue magazine à la Mexico.

Vuelta

Distributed by: EBSCO; Continental Book Co.

Magazine dealing with literature.

■ Newspapers

For patrons who want to keep up with news from home, the following Web site lists "All the World's Newspapers," organized by country: http://www.on-linenewpapers.com

Ethnic News Watch is put out by SoftLine Information, Inc. (http://www.slinfo.com) and is a bilingual database of the complete text of newspapers, magazines, and other publications from the ethnic, minority, and native press. Available by subscription.

For more Internet newspaper listings see Chapter 7. It would also be appropriate to subscribe to one or two actual newspapers from the countries of origin of your patrons, and/or subscribe to a local Spanish-language newspaper.

■ Computers

Because 25 percent of Hispanics do not have telephones, at least that many do not have access to the World Wide Web either because it is accessible over phone lines (Mellander 1998). The situation may change as Web TV becomes more prevalent, but patrons will still need information on how to use that medium effectively. Some libraries have found that programs for making greeting cards and posters entice patrons in to use the computers and could serve as a nonthreatening introduction to computer literacy. Self-paced software-based tutorials for learning English are also popular.

Several of the dealers listed in Appendix C carry computer books and/or software.

■ Other Resources

New Americans Initiative, Fannie Mae Foundation

> 4000 Wisconsin Ave., NW
> North Tower, Suite 1
> Washington, D.C. 20016-2804
> 202-274-8087 or 202-274-8095
> http://www.fanniemaefoundation.org/partner/indexb.htm.

>> Offers free material on home ownership in several languages including Spanish.

Ethnic NewsWatch

> SoftLine Information, Inc.
> 20 Summer St., Stamford
> CT 06901; 1-800-524-7922

■ Works Cited

Abramoff, Carolann and Loraine Cors. Personal interview with author, 13 March 1999.

Adelante: Recommendations for Effective Library Service to the Spanish-Speaking. The California State Library Task Force on Serving Spanish-Speaking Communities, 1994.

Alire, Camila and Orlando Archibeque. *Serving Latino Communities: A How-To-Do-It Manual for Librarians*. New York: Neal-Schuman, 1998.

Castro, Rafaela. Assessment of Ethnic Collections. In *Developing Library Collections for California's Emerging Majority: A Manual of Resources for Ethnic Collection Development*, edited by Katharine Scarborough. Berkeley, Calif.: University of California, Berkeley School of Library and Information Studies, 1990.

Chao, Sheau-yueh J. "The New Americans Program: Queens Borough Public Library's Service to Multilingual/Multicultural Communities," *Public Libraries* (Nov.-Dec. 1993): 319–322.

DeHerrera, Maria. Personal interview with author, 31 Oct. 1998.

Everett, Peter. Personal communication, 11 May 1998.

Gilbert, Deborah. "Migrant Workers Learn 'Survival English' from U-M Juniors and Seniors," *University of Michigan News & Info Services*. Sept. 1997. [Online] Available: http://www.umich.edu/~newsinfo/U_Record/Issues97/Sep3_97/migrant.htm (Accessed: Jan. 26, 1999).

Gonzalez, Christine. Telephone Interview, 28 Sept. 1998.

Güereña, Salvador, editor. *Latino Librarianship: A Handbook for Professionals*. Jefferson, N.C.: McFarland, 1990.

Güereña, Salvador and Vivian Pisano. *Latino Periodicals*. Jefferson, N.C.: McFarland, 1998.

Latin American Literature Pathfinder. [Salt Lake City], Utah: Reforma de Utah, 1998.

Lynch, Mary Jo. "Using Public Libraries: What Makes a Difference?" *American Libraries* (Nov. 1997): 64, 66.

McCain, Nancy. "Final Report: Hablamos Español: Outreach and Inclusion." Lake County Public Library, Leadville, Colo., 1996. Photocopy.

McQuillan, Jeff and Lucy Tse. "Child Language Brokering in Linguistic Minority Communities: Effects on Cultural Interaction, Cognition, and Literacy," *Language and Education* 9 no. 3 (1995): 195–215.

Mellander, Gustavo A. and Nelly Mellander. "Distance Learning Closing In," *Hispanic Outlook* (18 Dec. 1998): 9–11.

Milo, Albert. Reference Service to the Spanish-Speaking. In *Latino Librarianship: A Handbook for Professionals*, edited by Salvador Güereña. Jefferson, N.C.: McFarland, 1990.

Mora, Pat. Conversation with author, Steamboat Springs, Colo., 12 Sept. 1998.

Morales, Diana. Telephone interview, 26 March 1999.

Morgan, Dawn-Leigh. "Se Habla Español," Hobbs, N.Mex. *News-Sun,* 1 May 1994, 17.

Ortiz, Margarita. Personal communication, 15 May 1998.

Patterson, Irania Macías. Telephone interview, 22 Jan. 1999.

Payne-Button, Linda. Telephone interview, 13 Oct. 1998.

Rey, Clara. Personal conversation, Taos, N.Mex., 31 Oct. 1998.

Rivera, Martín. Telephone interview, 24 July 1998.

Roslow, Peter and J.A.F. Nicholls. "Targeting the Hispanic Market: Comparative Persuasion of TV Commercials in Spanish and English," *Journal of Advertising Research* (May-June 1996): 67+.

Schon, Isabel. "Spanish-Language Books for Young Readers - Great Expectations, Disappointing Realities," *Booklist* (1 Oct. 1995): 318–319.

Shapiro, Michael. "What About the Library Market?" *Publishers Weekly* (25 Aug. 1997): S47.

Chapter 3

Kids Are Kids: Preschool to Early Elementary

■ Starting Early

Kids are kids are kids—around the world. They laugh, they cry, they behave, they're naughty, they get hungry and dirty, and they thrive on hugs and praise. From the day children are born, they begin the learning process that forms the basis for their lives' experiences. Although the sights and sounds that come to children's senses differ according to the specific culture of their families, they all serve the same purpose: facilitating the child's finding a place within society and becoming a fully-functioning, productive adult.

We all delight in a baby's babbling, encouraging sounds that approximate actual words. Whether we realize it or not, these are the foundations for literacy and reading, just as the oral story-telling traditions of our forefathers led to rich auditory expression and written records. For most children, these foundations help prepare them for school and more formal learning experiences upon which they can build.

But what happens when a child's earliest learning is in a language other than English, and that child has to begin formal schooling in this country without a solid base from which to start? That would be a rude awakening for any of us—like building a block tower, only to have one of the blocks on the bottom row pulled out. If the base is wide and strong enough, maybe it will remain upright; if the base is narrow, it will most likely crumple and fall.

47

At least one elementary school bilingual coordinator feels strongly that it is a form of oppression to deny children the opportunity to develop their first language because much of one's identity is wrapped up with that language. Cummins (1989) and others have shown that immersing children in their first language during their formative years is essential to give them the foundation for learning in general, and learning a second language (English) in particular. Once one has learned the basics of speaking, reading, and writing in any language, those skills are readily transferable to any other language. Learning in one's first language is really about literacy. Otherwise, children may end up illiterate in two languages.

Language Exposure

From the beginning, children need to be exposed to the richness of written and spoken language that comes from connecting with loving humans (Nathenson-Mejia 1994, 149–164). Staying at home with young children is an important value for Hispanic mothers and Schwartz (n.d.) reports that nearly one-half of them do so. Mothers cannot be faulted for keeping their children close during those early years, but as a result many do not have preschool experiences and are not exposed to the readiness activities with which other children are acquainted.

Besides working with day-care and preschool programs, libraries have an opportunity to offer enrichment to at-home preschoolers by encouraging moms to participate in library programs and showing them how they and their children will benefit from participation. If parents are monolingual Spanish-speakers, they may be embarrassed to enter a place where they will draw attention to themselves because of their inability to speak English well. As they are made to feel welcome, they need to be assured that speaking, reading, or singing to their children in Spanish will be only beneficial, not detrimental. Some parents erroneously feel that by not speaking Spanish they will help their children speak better English like "Americans," thus denying them a rich part of their heritage. Others may keep youngsters at home so they will be exposed to a minimum of English until they start school.

Alma Flor Ada (1998) has recounted a poignant story: As a college freshman in Denver, Colo., she did volunteer work with orphanages and would often tell stories to the children—sometimes in English, sometimes in Spanish. One time when she was telling a story in English, a little three-year-old girl said to her: "Please speak the other way." Asked why, because she did not speak Spanish, the child replied: "That's the way my mother used to sound." Children really can be wise beyond their years.

Collaboration

Getting the word out to at-home mothers or other caregivers about library programs may be an obstacle to overcome, especially if there are no older children in the family to take home notes or verbal messages from school. Many of the stay-at-home moms are not aware of the opportunities available to them in the community or that they are entitled to participate. This is where collaborative efforts with other community agencies may be especially beneficial.

Medical clinics in Colorado's San Luis Valley are participating in the Reach Out and Read program sponsored by the American Academy of Pediatrics (address at end of chapter). This program is targeted at children from ages six weeks to five years old, and the physicians, in addition to caring for physical needs, hand out free children's books for parents and write prescriptions (instructions) to read to their children for so many minutes each day. The fact that these professionals encourage reading is an incentive for parents to follow the prescription and give their children a solid foundation in reading. Hopefully the librarians in the area make sure they also have bilingual flyers to help families connect with other appropriate library programs.

Starting even before a child is born, the Carnegie Library of Pittsburgh, in conjunction with the American Library Association's "Born to Read" campaign, has a program of outreach to pregnant adolescents. As part of the young women's prenatal checkups and parenting classes, they are introduced to the values of reading (Barlow 1997, 20–22). These same activities could also be used as part of high school parenting classes.

The A. K. Smiley Public Library in Redlands, Calif., presents a booklet of pre-reading activities (available in English and Spanish) to parents of all newborns (Burgess 1998). During home visits in Bensenville, Ill., part of their Community of Readers project, new parents are presented with a bag of materials including a board book or paperback book, handmade puppet, and material from Baby TALK (address at end of chapter). Reading advocates take this opportunity to encourage the family to participate and to complete their library card applications (Rodriguez and Tejeda 1993, 331–335). The Aurora (Ill.) Public Library works in conjunction with the Visiting Nurse Association to reach women with infants and offer them a free book to help promote reading (Aude 1998).

■ Preschool Story Hours

Even librarians who are not fluent in Spanish can read in that language with a little practice; it will get easier over time. It may help to have a fluent speaker give you pointers on your pronunciation. Listening to sitcoms on the local Spanish-language television station will also help accustom your ear to the sounds of the language. In reality, it is easier for a beginning reader to read in Spanish than

English because there are fewer variations to the vowel sounds and fewer exceptions to other pronunciation and spelling rules. If there is truly no one on the library staff who can master reading in Spanish, how about inviting some Spanish-speaking high school or college students or parents to read?

Lapsits for infants and toddlers, and story hours for older children, either at the library or at outreach sites, could encourage the participation of parents, helping reinforce the importance of the parents' role in their children's lives, and demonstrating effective techniques. Parents need to see the story hours or other library activities as complementing their parenting skills, not replacing them, and should be encouraged to check out library books to share at home. Even parents whose reading skills are poor or nonexistent may not yet realize that they can "read" by telling stories from the pictures in the book. Transportation might be provided to parents who cannot provide their own or where public transportation is inadequate.

As you get to know the moms who do bring children to story hours, you may be able to find some valuable helpers, but do not pressure them until they are ready to make that commitment. Perhaps two or three women who are friends would find it less intimidating to work together; perhaps their husbands need to be sold on the idea first so they will not be opposed to their wives leaving home for this activity. These assistants could bring their own treasury of traditional tales, finger-plays, and games that they learned as children and can teach these to the library staff as well as to the youngsters.

Once you have parents participating in programs at the library, do your best to minimize possible obstacles. One obstacle to borrowing library books for home use can be that parents are uncomfortable with the responsibility: they are unfamiliar with the practice of borrowing from a library, late fines may be seen as a form of punishment, and they may fear the costs of having to replace lost items on a limited budget.

Charlotte, North Carolina

Irania Macías Patterson, a storyteller hired by the Public Library of Charlotte and Mecklenburg County (N.C.) to work with the Latino population, writes of her experiences:

> My first question was how to start? . . . I knew the majority of the community (of new immigrants) was Mexican and I thought that being a Venezuelan could be a barrier; however, I quickly learned that if I showed them my true feelings for helping them improve their lives, and used my sense of humor to break the ice there were no barriers.
>
> In some countries in Latin America it is not common to have storytellers in the library and the title I received was: *Narradora de Cuentos* or Storyteller. At first the Hispanic parents thought:

"¿Una narradora de cuentos? Well I do not need that. I need a job first or health assistance."

They did not see the purpose of having a storyteller until I explained to them what it meant. For some low-income families, education is not a need. For them health or job opportunities are their priorities, so my job was to open their eyes and make them understand that education is a big need.

I had to make parents and preschoolers fall in love with reading, but storytelling was a concept they did not understand. These parents were never read to before as children, so why are they going to read to their children now? It was like telling someone who has never tried a mango, to eat it just because it is good!

I knew that until they understood what I was talking about, they would not get involved in the program, not come to the library. I took hundreds of flyers to advertise the program at health fairs, festivals, schools, churches, and organizations that target Hispanics, to contact some mothers first. I went on radio programs, and I wrote several articles in *La Noticia*, a local Hispanic newspaper. I found that personal contact was the best way to reach the population.

I contacted three mothers who lived in the most concentrated Hispanic areas of the county. They were assigned to be the leaders of their apartment complex and spread the word and they became known as the "Mom Leaders." We started in their homes with three children in each one and after a month we had approximately eight per home. Then one mother told another mother in another area of the city, and the phone began to ring. More and more parents were wondering what was going on in their friends' homes and they invited me to start a new group in their neighborhood. I never said "No"; I went to their houses and gathered the people close to their homes in one place to form bigger groups in the same areas. In March (1998), three months later, I had five regular programs done in the homes and two programs in the libraries.

How to Move the Families to the Libraries?

One time I had 13 children in one Mom Leader's home and only three parents had transportation. It was time to move them into the library, but I did not know how to do it. The space was small and the home environment did not offer the quality setting that a story time required: the telephone rang, a child wanted to pick up his toy under the sofa, the room was too cold or too hot, there was poor lighting, a mother had to cook because her husband was coming home soon—these were some of the problems I needed to resolve soon.

"Let's all take the bus to the library," I suggested, and we did.

It was and still is very hard to tell a mother who does not speak English, depends on her husband 100 percent, and who has two or three babies, to take a bus. It was an educational campaign that required a lot of psychology. Progressively, they understood the significance of their children's education and the little sacrifices they need to make. . . .

Some English-speaking parents want their children to learn Spanish through storytelling, but that's not my objective now. Some parents want their school-age children to go to storytelling, and it is very hard to tell them that at this point we just provided a program for preschoolers, however everybody is welcome to stay.

Sometimes I go to home daycare with Vietnamese, Cambodian, Hispanic, Russian or Chinese children. . . . What language am I going to use if they do not speak English and I only speak Spanish and English? In those moments I feel frustrated. Sometimes it is fascinating to see children who do not speak the same language participating and listening. It is a challenge and due to these factors I always have on hand all types of book ideas and games. I have to be prepared for anything.

Teaching English

I do use an ESL approach as part of my storytelling session. Storytelling is an excellent strategy to teach any language especially when the story is highly predictable, includes vocabulary representing the home and school environment, is repetitive, makes use of patterns like those found in *Brown Bear, Brown Bear What Do You See?*, and lends itself to heavy use of visuals to illustrate its content and progress.

If the child does not speak English I tell the story in Spanish first and progressively, later, in English. Sometimes the visuals are so good that it is not necessary to use Spanish at all. (This article was adapted from one written by Irania Macías Patterson and used with permission of *North Carolina Libraries*, *the Professional Journal of the North Carolina Library Association*.)

Although the Latino population in Charlotte is somewhat transient, Patterson has met with some groups for one and one-half to two years. Hostessing a group of their peers is a nonthreatening activity for the mothers and gets them involved from the beginning. Once families have become familiar with the at-home story hours they are more comfortable going to the library itself for programs. Ideas for story-hour themes can often be found in Latino arts and crafts books.

Tucson, Arizona

Rebecca Tellez Pombo (1998), Bilingual School Librarian for Harriet Johnson Primary School in Tucson, Arizona, explains the methods she uses with her students:

> My school has many bilingual classrooms, so I use the Preview-Review method for instruction or reading a story. I will introduce the book in English if the book is in Spanish and then do a quick review in English after the story. I try to stay in just one language during these times. My library's Spanish collection is fully integrated with the rest of the collection. The Spanish books are identified by a fluorescent yellow dot on the spine. This way, the children don't view the Spanish literature as different and separate, but as part of the whole. Also, they are more free to check out books in the language they want.

Miami, Florida

Lucía González (1999), a librarian with the Miami-Dade Public Library System as well as an author, uses the following routine in her Spanish-language children's story times. She begins with a counting song in which the children can participate, reads a book relevant to their lives, tells rhymes or riddles with which the group can participate, tells an oral folk tale, reads another book, and ends with a game and more songs. She has also helped create a traveling puppeteering troupe, *Colorín Colorado,* which other librarians could duplicate in English or Spanish. The scripts she has developed are available from the Miami-Dade Public Library.

If the library is short-staffed, perhaps a group of older students could present bilingual puppet shows or skits. Make sure the puppets, dolls, and other toys used as part of library programs represent different skin colors and ethnicities.

■ What Children Need

Don't be surprised if the behavior of some Latino children is different from the behavior of other children who come to the library. Even though all children have the same basic needs, their early experiences may have been different. If both parents work and preschoolers are being left in the care of older siblings, they may be dirtier or louder than you would like. They may be attempting to deal (perhaps not very effectively) with culture shock, or be missing family members and friends who stayed behind in the home country. The subtle nonverbal clues by which people of each society size up situations have changed so the children are constantly having to reassess everything around them, even things that used to be simple like going to the store for Mom. They may have come from war-torn countries where they experienced disturbing events, or be seeing depressed parents who are having trouble coping with transitions that are harder than expected.

Igoa (1993, 99) pointed out that when a child's cultural identity is challenged, that child may retreat into silence, academic failure, and escape hatches. Children may feel that as soon as they step out the door, the values they have learned at home are left behind and they are in another world with different values. Teachers and librarians need to show these children how to adapt to the new culture and new set of expectations without abandoning or devaluing important family standards. On the other hand, many adults find it enjoyable to work with immigrant Latino children because they have been taught to be obedient and respectful of adults.

Unfortunately, some teachers report that dark-skinned, poor, Spanish-speaking children are still not treated as well as European immigrants who are lighter skinned and speak a more prestigious language like French. When I asked why a bilingual kindergarten classroom with a physically challenged student had no classroom aide, while another classroom with only English-speaking students in the same school system, did, I was told that some children generate more value for services. We need to be careful that these kinds of actions do not speak louder than our words when we say that regardless of ethnicity, every student is of equal value. It is easy for children to pick up on these subtle messages about how we perceive their worth in our society.

Learning to Read

The reading needs of Spanish-speaking pre-emergent and emergent readers are really no different than the needs of any other children—they just need to be in Spanish, with characters and situations to which they can relate. As children listen to stories, and then begin telling their own, they are practicing any number of skills. By listening, they learn to discriminate speech sounds: *spot* versus *pot*, or *pecado* (sin) versus *pescado* (fish), and learn the correct rhythm and structure of the language. They get to hear and practice different patterns of rhyme and begin to appreciate the nuances of language. Spanish tends to be a more musical language than English, so it would be a shame for children to miss the chance to hear and appreciate that richness.

There seems to be more Spanish-language material for the preschool and beginning reader age groups than any other, so finding books for the library should not be a problem. Remember, however, that an alphabet book in English will not serve Spanish-speakers. "A" may be for apple in English, but it's "M" for *manzana* in Spanish. If you use a mixture of English and Spanish because your language skills are limited, or you have a mixed group of children, use lots of body language, hands-on activities, movement, acting out, visuals, and music to make the story understandable to both language groups. This would be a great time to use origami or folded cutout figures to hold the children's interest.

Using a favorite story several times with the same group of children would allow for telling it sometimes with more English words, and other times with more Spanish. That way children of both language groups are learning from the other. Be empathetic if children do not understand; you would be frustrated too if you did not know what was going on, but everyone thought you should.

Picture books with imaginative pictures of children who look like them allow children to exercise their own imaginations, and practice verbal and storytelling skills. When there are no printed words, library patrons from any number of language backgrounds can use the same books effectively. Picture books can also be used to teach counting skills and the related number symbols that are the same in English and Spanish even if the number names are different.

As children begin to learn the alphabet and sight-reading, big books allow them to follow along as someone else reads. They learn that the language spoken at home also has meaning in print. Fairy and folk tales from a variety of cultures can be used with children of all backgrounds to help them appreciate the similarities between peoples and the richness of other cultures.

Poetry introduces children to the music of language, as do nursery rhymes, songs, games, and chants. Predictable books or stories with repetitious phrases allow the children to participate by repeating the phrase at the appropriate place. Even for adults who are fluent in Spanish, these phrases can be even more tongue twisting than "Peter Piper picked a peck of pickled peppers," but can lead to some good laughs between you and the children. The youngsters will probably delight in saying them better than you do (Tinajero and Huerta-Macías 1993, 258).

Materials Selection

For materials acquisition, Beth Elder (1998) of the Denver Public Library advises using one's knowledge of children's literature in general, and then just jumping in and being experimental. She does not always rely on reviews, but does peruse publishers' catalogs to see what is new, and tries to select appropriate books with which children will be successful, and which parents will enjoy reading to them. She suggests starting with translations of such familiar books as Disney and The Magic School Bus and seeing if they are used. She does not feel pressured to buy a book on every topic if she cannot find the quality she wants.

Although the children will want to read, or hear, their favorites in Spanish translations, be careful not to get books in which the Spanish translations use English syntax and patterns. It is also important to find some stories that are original to the Latino cultures represented by participating children, to be shared with all children at story hours. The criteria for book selection listed in Chapter 4 will help with the purchase of material for this level also, as will consultation with publishers and distributors listed in Appendix C.

Storytelling

Spanish-language or bilingual storytellers can be great additions to library programs for all ages. As a children's librarian, you may be a storyteller who could turn some stories into bilingual ones, or perhaps you know of another storyteller in your community who could do so. In our community we have received grant funds through LSCA and the local chapter of the International Reading Council to secure bilingual storytellers, who were a great hit with teachers and kids alike. After getting to know your Latino population, however, you could discover grandparents or other retired senior citizens who, with a little training, could develop a talent in telling traditional tales, or stories from the "olden days" when they were a child.

Beginning readers benefit from listening to audiocassettes of stories while they look at the words and pictures in accompanying books. Some of these sets are available commercially, but you could also make your own book/tape sets by having older students or other volunteers record favorite Spanish stories you already have in the library.

As a variation of this theme, the Forsyth County Public Library in Winston-Salem, North Carolina has presented a Spanish-language story time on a local radio station using audiotapes from the library's collection (Sundell 1999). They find that they may have to begin paying for airtime, but perhaps they could find a local bookstore or other business willing to support this effort. The Montrose (Colo.) Public Library has a telephone system that allows them to provide an English and Spanish storyline—also known as "Dial a Story" or "Tele Cuento." They record their own stories and try to change them once a week. Their challenge has been finding native Spanish-speakers who would be willing to record stories for them because the Spanish-speakers often do not want to call attention to themselves. Using folk and fairy tales that are in the public domain would be the least likely to cause any copyright problems (Oslund 1999).

■ History of Spanish Children's Literature

The best history of children's literature in the Spanish-speaking world that I found was by Alma Flor Ada (1993, 107–115), whom I thank for the information in this section. All literature began with an oral tradition as people of all cultures told stories to pass long winter nights, sought explanations for events they did not totally understand, or expressed feelings. Over the centuries, the Iberian Peninsula experienced conquests by and immigrations of a number of peoples—Romans, Visigoths, Muslims, Jews, Christians—each adding unique elements to stories handed down from one generation to the next. Later, in the seventeenth and eighteenth centuries, Perrault in France and the Brothers Grimm in Germany began recording many of the spoken folk tales in written form, but no one in the Spanish-speaking world did the same for that body of folk tradition. Although Spain did publish a number of adult books in the nineteenth century, there were no children's writers there or in Latin America. José Martí published the only significant children's literature in Spanish during that century in New York while he was there in exile.

Efforts at promoting children's books at the beginning of the twentieth century were hampered by the legacy of colonialism and Third World poverty left in Central and South America, and by the totalitarian regime of Generalísimo Franco following the Spanish Civil War. Books written in Latin America were mainly distributed within their countries of origin while translations of books from Europe and North America were much more readily available to Latin-American children. Following Franco's death in 1975, publishing in Spain revived. Spanish publishers, especially those in Barcelona where the people historically spoke Catalán, are more aware of bilingual, bicultural issues. With their proximity to the rest of Europe, Spanish publishers have also translated and published quality children's literature from those countries. In more recent years, the quality and amount of children's literature has greatly increased throughout the Spanish-speaking world, so selection has become an easier task. Children now have a better chance of finding books that deal with situations, places, and people with which they are familiar. However, there is still much that could be done.

■ Family Literacy

Family Literacy programs can provide for the needs of preschoolers and their parents. The programs can take a variety of forms, depending on the needs of the participants, and can include such components as Spanish literacy, ESL and/or GED for parents, while addressing children's reading readiness skills.

At The Center, a day-care facility in Leadville, Colorado, the Family Literacy Coordinator holds monthly meetings with participating families (Osius 1998). In an informal setting over pizza and soft drinks, parents see reading activities modeled and discuss interactive reading methods: how to read and discuss the story, how to ask questions to involve children in the reading process, how to encourage youngsters to make up their own variations to tell to their stuffed animals or grandparents. The children get to borrow book boxes (available in Spanish and English) with such items as puzzles, math games, puppets, and fun reading materials and receive a book they can keep. Return of the boxes and missing pieces has not been a problem, possibly because the participants have developed a mutually respectful relationship with the coordinator. Another agency in the community offers parenting classes in Spanish to which parents can be referred.

Mulhern (1994) suggests having parents create a home literacy center for children with such supplies as crayons, pencils, scissors, paper (white and colored), magazine pictures, glue, and blank notebooks. Perhaps area stores would donate some of the materials. Local businesses with discarded computer printouts might be willing to donate the paper so children could draw pictures on the clean backs. Parents in the program could discuss ways to use the collected materials with their children and show off children's creations at meetings.

The Pajaro Valley Literacy Project has been described in several publications and serves to show how a program originally aimed at school children can have tremendous impact on the whole family. After seeing the interest with which Alma Flor Ada was received in a "Meet the Author" program, the California school district decided to expand the program into one for parents aimed at strengthening interactions between parents and children, and between home and school. Children's literature was chosen as a nonthreatening topic, and parents were issued personal (written and face-to-face) invitations to the programs. The enthusiasm that Ada contributed to the topic undoubtedly added to the success of the program, and parents learned the wonderful features books can offer, to themselves and to their children. As a result, children were encouraged to write their own stories that parents read during group sessions, and adults and children gained in oral reading and speaking skills. For some parents this was the first time they had seen their children's talents affirmed (Brown 1993, 180–183; Cummins 1989, 80–83; and Ada 1988).

Orellana (1996) describes a similar program in the Los Angeles area where a book was produced from the stories families wrote. Each family received a copy of the book that was also distributed to local libraries, classrooms, and other community organizations. What a great way to show people that one does not have to be rich and famous to have a valid story to tell and to preserve local history.

In any Family Literacy program parents need to see that their personal goals are being addressed; that they themselves are valuable resources who are provided with information and resources to encourage their children's success; that their home language skills are valued and that they are encouraged to share literacy experiences in that language at home (Mulhern, Rodriguez-Brown, and Shanahan 1994).

■ Successful Programs

Nancy Tabor (1999), a bilingual early elementary teacher who grew up in Mexico and the United States, found a new avocation when she became frustrated at the lack of colorful Spanish-language materials to use in her classroom. At her daughter's suggestion, she wrote her own book, using bright construction paper cutouts for illustrations. Other teachers were attracted to her homemade book, so Tabor took it to a publisher to see about having more copies made to distribute (that was before color photocopiers were readily available). That contact led to an offer to publish that book and others to fill the niche.

Even though Tabor does not see herself as an artist, she says, "There are a million ways to do illustrations," and she has made use of many of them to illustrate her culturally sensitive books. She is also careful not to have too much text crowding the pages of her bilingual books because she feels that can intimidate people not used to books and reading. At present, with the increasing prevalence of color copiers, student- or teacher-made books can much more easily be copied for distribution to the students themselves, or school or public libraries.

With the help of Silvia Diez and Aida Fernández (1999), teachers in the Miami-Dade County Public Schools, students have created some wonderful books of their own. Younger students can create alphabet books using Spanish words for common objects from home or school to represent the different letters. The two women made sure the end results were attractive so the children and their families realized the value of the books and the efforts that went into creating them.

Early "books" consist of worksheets on which children fill in blanks about their families or neighborhoods. The pages of more advanced books might be in the shape of a particular animal or object and have the colorful covers laminated for protection. The teachers also recommend that students write about themes or experiences they can share with their parents, such as parents' favorite toys as children, important family events, or why the child was given a particular name. Even if families cannot afford to purchase books, those the children create, and of which they are proud, could help develop an appreciation for books and the children's talents.

The libraries in Alamosa serve a primarily rural area of south central Colorado with one of the highest percentages of Hispanics in the state, many of them retired citizens. Julie Herrera, Library Media Specialist for the school district's elementary schools and Margaret Morris of the Southern Peaks Public Library (1997), secured grant funding through the Colorado State Library to begin a "Spellbinders" storytelling program (address below) for students in prekindergarten through fifth grade. One of the goals of the project was to foster intergenerational communication so students could "gain an understanding of the way things were and why we do things the way we do." Herrera, who is already a professional storyteller, conducted half-day workshops on "Choosing Appropriate Material," "Reading Aloud," "Telling Someone Else's Story," and "Telling

Your Own Stories." A fee of $25.00 was charged for the workshops, however, scholarships (provided for with the grant money) were given to those who could not afford that amount, and the fee was returned to participants who completed the workshops as well as honored their commitment to present at least three stories. Following the end of the grant period, Morris and Herrera planned to continue meeting monthly with the storyteller volunteers to evaluate their efforts, and attempt to recruit more people.

Successful programs at the Bensenville (Ill.) Community Public Library have included "Stories and Songs for Babies" (for parents and infants) and "Stories and Songs with Grands" (for grandparents and preschoolers). Taking story programs to health clinics where they coincide with Well-Baby clinics would be another way to hook families not accustomed to visiting libraries (Rodriguez and Tejeda 1993, 331–335).

At the Tucson-Pima Public Library (Ariz.), a story hour for hearing-impaired children also serves nonhearing-impaired Latino children. Because the hearing-impaired children "get into" the signed story, the Latinos do as well, bringing bilingualism to a different level (Rivera 1998). Librarians in Florida who offer story hours to children of migrant farm workers find they need to schedule the story hours on Sunday mornings when the parents do not work. If there is no other place to hold these story hours, they pitch a large tent in a central location (Abramoff and Cors 1999).

In Houston, a Mexican physician asked a bilingual middle school teacher if he could tutor his four-year-old son on manners. That contact resulted in the teacher volunteering his time to work with 15 or so preschoolers on their social skills. The class, which was conducted mostly in Spanish, met for at least two months and was very popular (Morales 1999).

For summer reading programs, some public libraries try to tap the services of bilingual teachers and classroom aides. Because they are usually not on contract with the school district during the summer, school personnel could be valuable temporary additions to the library staff. In Littleton, Colorado, East Elementary School offers an ESL Literacy Club for first and second graders that meets once a week during the school year.

Some libraries use software geared toward preschool children and have conducted successful computer literacy programs for preschoolers and their parents. The children would be hooked by the bright animations, and the parents would learn to manipulate the computer with a nonthreatening program.

■ Periodicals

Although there really are not any good Spanish-language periodical titles for preschoolers that I could find available in the United States, except for the four-page newspaper put out by Scholastic, the following list includes some of the parenting magazines available.

Addresses of Distributors

EBSCO, International Headquarters
  PO Box 11943
  Birmingham, AL 35201-1943

Latin American Periodicals
  2555 N. Coyote Dr., Suite 109
  Tucson, AZ 85745

Periodical Titles

Padres de Sesame Street

Children's Television Workshop
  1 Lincoln Plaza
  New York, NY 10023

> A parenting magazine put out by the Sesame Street people.

Padres e Hijos

Distributed by: EBSCO; Latin American Periodicals
  Subscriptions: Service Dept.
  P.O. Box 37253
  Boone, IA 50037-0253

> Although the practical articles deal primarily with pregnancy, infancy, and the preschool years, this monthly parenting magazine covers children up to the pre-adolescent years.

Parent and Preschooler Newsletter

North Shore Child & Family Guidance Center
  480 Westbury Rd.
  Roslyn Heights, NY 11577-2215
  Distributed by: EBSCO

> "A monthly exploration of early childhood topics from The Lindner Early Childhood Training Institute," this newsletter is available in English, or, for a slightly higher subscription fee, in combination with Spanish. Although perhaps a little advanced for parents with minimal education, the newsletter does offer practical suggestions for those wanting to provide optimal developmental opportunities for preschoolers. Line drawings show parents and children of varying ethnic backgrounds.

Ranger Rick Magazine: http://nwf.org/nwf/rrick/index.html

> From the main page, click on *Artículos en Español* to read several of the month's articles in Spanish.

Scholastic® Classroom Magazines: http://www.scholastic.com

> Scholastic® News en Español
> P.O. Box 3710
> Jefferson City, MO 65102-3710
> Distributed by: EBSCO

>> Although geared for use in a classroom setting, the three levels (Grades 1–3) of *Scholastic® News en Español*, published weekly during the school year, could be used as supplemental material in a school library, especially where there is no bilingual or Spanish-language instruction. Teachers ordering 10 or more copies will receive a free Teacher's Guide. For preschool and kindergarten students, Scholastic publishes *Let's Find Out (Spanish)*. The colorful four-page issues of *Let's Find Out* encourage young students to explore and discuss their worlds.

■ Other Resources

Storytelling

Spellbinders

> P.O. Box 128
> Woody Creek, CO 81656
> 970-923-1230; Fax: 970-923-2396

>> For information on starting a Spellbinders program, contact this organization.

National Storytelling Membership Association

> 116 1/2 West Main St.
> Jonesborough, TN 37659
> 1-800-525-4514
> http://www.storynet.org

>> The Web site does give information about member storytellers, some of whom tell Spanish and/or bilingual stories.

Outreach to Parents

Selections Book Fairs, Inc.

> 3558 North High St.
> Columbus, OH 43214
> 1-800-551-5885
>
> *Lectura y Escritura: Donde Comienza la Educación: Ayudando a Sus Hijos En El Hogar = Reading and Writing: Where It All Begins: Helping Your Children at Home.* A booklet of about 40 pages published by the Literacy Connection in Spanish and English, showing pre-reading activities for preschoolers. The booklet can be purchased in bulk by schools and libraries.

Baby TALK, Inc.

> 1314 North Main
> Decatur, IL 62526
> http://www.babytalk.org
>
> "Baby TALK is a community effort designed to encourage parents in the nurturing of their small children. It is a collaborative effort of school districts, libraries, hospitals, health departments, and literacy projects. . . . Baby TALK has been serving parents and young children since 1986."

Reach Out and Read

> American Academy of Pediatrics, Dept. of Government Liaison
> 601 13th St., NW
> Washington, D.C. 20005
> http://www.aap.org
>
> Targeting children ages six weeks to five years, this program links health care and literacy.

Born to Read Project/Association for Library Service to Children

> 50 E. Huron St.
> Chicago, IL 60611
> http://www.ala.org/alsc/born.html
>
> "Born to Read builds partnerships between librarians and health care providers to reach out to new and expectant "at-risk" parents and help them raise children who are 'born to read.'"

Reading Is Fundamental, Inc. (RIF)

>600 Maryland Ave., SW, Suite 600, Smithsonian Institution
>Washington, D.C. 20024

>RIF offers a number of programs for the beginning reader: Family of Readers is a family reading program; Shared Beginnings gives teen parents skills to develop their children's reading readiness; Running Start and Books on the Menu are for beginning readers with the latter pairing fifth or sixth graders with kindergarteners and first graders for book sharing; Read With Me Videos offer tips for effectively reading with a preschooler. Although not developed especially for Spanish-speaking children and their families, they would be easily adaptable for this population.

Literacy Programs

National Center for Family Literacy (NCFL)

>Waterfront Plaza, Suite 200
>325 W. Main St.
>Louisville, KY 40202-4251; 502-584-1133
>http://www.famlit.org

>NCFL is an organization providing leadership for creating family literacy programs, encouraging other existing programs in this area and influencing public policy.

Center for Literacy

>University of Illinois at Chicago
>1040 W. Harrison (M/C 147)
>Chicago, IL 60607
>312-996-3013

>Has sets of nine different titles of brochures for parents in either English or Spanish dealing with literacy issues, and helping one's children.

Even Start Family Literacy Initiative

>Compensatory Education Programs, Office of Elementary and Secondary Education, U.S. Department of Education
>400 Maryland Ave., S. W.
>Washington, D.C. 20202-6132

>Even Start is a federally funded program to improve educational opportunities for low-income families by integrating early childhood education, adult literacy, and parenting education.

■ Works Cited

Abramoff, Carolann and Loraine Cors. Personal conversation with author, 13 March 1999.

Ada, Alma Flor. Contemporary Trends in Children's Literature Written in Spanish in Spain and Latin America. In *The Power of Two Languages: Literacy and Biliteracy for Spanish-Speaking Students*, edited by Josefina Villamil Tinajero and Alma Flor Ada. New York: Macmillan McGraw-Hill School Publishing, 1993.

————. The Pajaro Valley Experience. In *Minority Education: From Shame to Struggle*, edited by Tove Skutnabb-Kangas and Jim Cummins. Clevedon, Avon, England: Multilingual Matters Ltd., 1988, 223–238.

————. Personal interview, Denver, Colo., 24 April 1998.

Aude, Laurie. Personal communication, 12 June 1998.

Barlow, Cara. "Ooooh Baby, What a Brain!" *School Library Journal*, 43 (July 1997): 20–22.

Brown, Kristin. Balancing the Tools of Technology with Our Own Humanity: The Use of Technology in Building Partnerships and Communities. In *The Power of Two Languages: Literacy and Biliteracy for Spanish-Speaking Students*, edited by Josefina Villamil Tinajero and Alma Flor Ada. New York: Macmillan McGraw-Hill School Publishing, 1993.

Burgess, Larry. Telephone interview, 6 Oct. 1998.

Cummins, Jim. *Empowering Minority Students.* Sacramento, Calif.: California Association for Bilingual Education, 1989.

Diez, Silvia and Aida Fernández. *Como Elevar la Capacidad de Aprendizaje del Estudiante a Través de las Artes del Lenguaje en Español.* Presentation given at Annual International Bilingual/Multicultural Education Conference, National Association of Bilingual Education, 29 Jan. 1999, Denver, Colo.

Elder, Beth. Conversation with author, Denver, Colo., 4 May 1998.

González, Lucía. *Cultural Integration at the Library.* Presentation given at the Trejo Foster Foundation Hispanic Library Education Institute, 12 March 1999, Tampa, Fla. Published in: *Library Services to Youth of Hispanic Heritage*, edited by Barbara Immroth and Kathleen de la Peña McCook. Jefferson, N.C.: McFarland, 2000.

Herrera, Julie and Margaret Morris. Request for Proposal: *Let's Collaborate? Challenge to Improve Learning Through Library Partnerships.* (Alamosa Public Schools, Alamosa, Colo., 1997, photocopy).

Igoa, Cristina. Second Language Literacy and Immigrant Children: The Inner World of the Immigrant Child. In *The Power of Two Languages: Literacy and Biliteracy for Spanish-Speaking Students*, edited by Josefina Villamil Tinajero and Alma Flor Ada. New York: Macmillan McGraw-Hill School Publishing, 1993.

Morales, Diana. Telephone conversation with author, 26 March 1999.

Mulhern, Margaret, Flora V. Rodriguez-Brown, and Timothy Shanahan. "Family Literacy for Language Minority Families: Issues for Program Implementation," *NCBE Program Information Guide Series,* Number 17, Summer 1994. [Online] Available: http://www.ncbe.gwu.edu/ncbepubs/pigs/pig17.htm (Accessed Dec. 12, 1998).

Nathenson-Mejia, Sally. "Bridges Between Home and School: Literacy Building Activities for Non Native English Speaking Homes," *The Journal of Educational Issues of Language Minority Students* (Winter 1994): 149–164.

Orellana, Marjorie Faulstich. "¡Aquí Vivimos!: Voices of Central American and Mexican Participants in a Family Literacy Project," *The Journal of Educational Issue of Language Minority Students* (Summer 1996).[Online] Available: http://www.ncbe.gwu.edu/miscpubs/jeilms/vol/6/jeilms/608.htm.

Osius, Lucy. Personal conversation, Leadville, Colo., 18 Sept. 1998.

Oslund, Janet. Telephone conversation with author, 24 March 1999.

Patterson, Irania Macías. "The Public Library of Charlotte and Mecklenburg County Speaks Español," *North Carolina Libraries, the Professional Journal of the North Carolina Library Association* 56 (Winter 1998): 145–147.

Pombo, Rebecca Tellez. Personal communication, 14 May 1998.

Rivera, Martín. Telephone conversation with author, 10 Nov. 1998.

Rodriguez, Jill and Maria Tejeda. "Serving Hispanics Through Family Literacy: One Family at a Time," *Illinois Libraries* (Fall 1993): 331–335.

Schwartz, Wendy. "Hispanic Preschool Education: An Important Overview," *ERIC Digest.* Urbana, Ill.: ERIC Clearinghouse on Urban Education, n.d.

Sundell, Jon. Personal conversation, Tampa, Fla., 13 March 1999.

Tabor, Nancy. *Enhancing Cultural Awareness Through Children's Books.* Presentation given at Annual International Bilingual/Multicultural Education Conference, National Association of Bilingual Education, 28 Jan. 1999, Denver, Colo.

Tinajero, Josefina Villamil and Ana Huerta-Macías. Enhancing the Skills of Emergent Writers Acquiring English. In *The Power of Two Languages: Literacy and Biliteracy for Spanish-Speaking Students,* edited by Josefina Villamil Tinajero and Alma Flor Ada. New York: Macmillan McGraw-Hill School Publishing, 1993.

Chapter 4

Reading to Learn: The Middle Grades

■ Struggle for Literacy

We hope that children beyond the early elementary grades have mastered the fundamentals of reading, and although they will continue to work on reading skills, they will also use those skills to learn content in other subject areas. Latino immigrants who have had the chance to master reading concepts in Spanish will be more prepared to read in English and to comprehend more abstract ideas presented in that language.

Unfortunately, Spanish-speakers born in this country and constantly surrounded by English are often caught in a clash of cultures. They learn from an early age that the Spanish language and Latino cultures are of lesser value in our society and, with the resulting devaluation of their very identities, tend to do less well in their studies (Cummins 1989, 58). Minority students with good educational foundations in the home country who immigrate to the United States around 10 years of age or older often do better academically than Spanish-speakers born in this country because they have had a solid beginning in identity formation.

On the other hand, however, students coming from poverty-stricken or war-torn areas of the world where education is deficient or sporadic may not have the strong foundation from which to launch into English-language studies.

In addition, U.S. schools that offer bilingual classes to the early grades may not make adequate provisions for the education of monolingual students who do not arrive until the fifth or sixth grades when many bilingual programs are ready to transition students into English-only classrooms. The result can be that because of deficiencies in English and other academic skills, Latino students are over-age for the grade to which they are assigned—not conducive to their retention and success (Sosa 1993, 35).

Situational Literacy

Considering situational literacy is more easily acquired than academic literacy, a child's fluency in conversational English may give the erroneous impression that the child is ready to tackle all learning in that language (McQuillin and Tse 1995). However, for youngsters who develop conversational skills quickly, a breakdown in communication may start to occur around the fourth to sixth grades when these children are expected to grasp more and more difficult subject concepts with English that is insufficiently developed for academic rigor and without basic knowledge of specific subject areas in their first language.

At the same time they gain a superficial fluency in English conversation, youngsters may, if not given encouragement, lose the ability to use their home language. In their zeal to be "American," young people may overembrace the U.S. culture, losing the many positive attributes of their first culture. Conversations with parents and family may become limited to such exchanges as: "You want hamburger?" "Yeah." It may take many more years for the whole family to become fluent in English, so if children lose their ability to communicate effectively in their first language, it becomes difficult, if not impossible, to converse about such abstract topics as death or God—value-laden subjects that are important for parents to discuss with their children and that help youngsters understand their identities within the context of their cultural heritage.

Bilingual Literacy

Although many of us middle- and upper-class non-Latino parents spend good money sending our children to colleges and universities to learn a second language, the benefits of bilingualism for those whose first language is not English are often not recognized. However inadvertently, we encourage Latino students to forget their Spanish as they learn English. How much more advantageous it would be for students to learn two or more languages well from childhood and be able to benefit from future job opportunities that call for bilingual employees (Mora 1998). Our U.S. society does not look down on Europeans who are fluent in several languages, so why do we have a different standard for Hispanics? To put a monetary value on the skill of bilingualism, Jim Cummins (1999) estimated that it would cost a business a sum of at least $10,000 in instructional fees to make a monolingual executive fluent in a second language.

Libraries can encourage the maintenance of Spanish in Spanish-speaking students by providing a wide range of Spanish-language fiction and nonfiction, even if students are not receiving school instruction in that language. Even when children are ready and willing to read in English, they may still wish to read in Spanish and should be encouraged to do so, perhaps during periods of Sustained Silent Reading (SSR). At other times, either in the school or public library, Spanish-speakers can read together in small groups, on their own or with the help of older Spanish-speaking students or adult volunteers.

Students should be introduced to appropriate literature in both languages that will foster a love of reading. They need to read (in both languages) about characters who are dealing with and finding solutions to many of the same big and small problems the students themselves are encountering. When any second-language learner (adult or child) is ready to read in the less familiar language (English in this case), the content should be interesting (visually and content-wise) and culturally relevant, and needs to be introduced in a low-anxiety setting (Allen 1987, 33; Tse 1996).

Some teachers have mentioned that it is difficult to get youngsters to take books home from the school or public library, because it is not an activity to which they are accustomed. However, with the encouragement of teachers and librarians, they soon love it. Many immigrant families do not read for pleasure but only when they need information, so parents themselves may not model reading behavior at home. Nevertheless, the parents need to be shown that their interest and involvement with their children's reading is vital. Assigning students to read to a parent each night from their selected book(s) can lead to major improvements in reading skills (Cummins 1989, 62). We should help parents realize that even if they do not speak English, reading practice in Spanish can be of at least as much value for the child as reading in English.

Brokering

McQuillin and Tse (1995) showed that children who engage in brokering (interpreting communication for others who do not understand the new language in spoken or written form) develop higher levels of cognitive and linguistic abilities in both languages than children who do not broker. Although this ability may not be reflected in school achievement because it involves situational rather than academic literacy, children who broker often mature earlier with greater self-confidence and independence, have broader cultural understanding, and acculturate sooner. They may also take on responsibility for making their own decisions earlier than other students who do not broker because it is easier to do so than trying to explain the nuances of a particular situation to a parent who does not yet have a good grasp of U.S. customs.

Even though the ability to broker may engender some negative feelings such as added stress from the increased responsibility, and embarrassment, frustration, or resentment toward family members (including parents) who cannot speak adequate English, the talents of these students could be used to the advantage of the library while giving the students a recognized, valued role. As mentioned in Chapter 3, it is essential to affirm these students and the positive cultural experiences and knowledge they bring from which everyone can benefit. It is also important to celebrate the knowledge and talents parents or other relatives bring to the community so the young people do not come to think of them as ignorant, country bumpkins whom they can ignore if they do not like their old-fashioned advice. These family members could be recruited for volunteer tasks during down times between seasonal employment opportunities.

As with any patron who enters the public library for the first time, children need to be welcomed with a smile and made to feel at home, even if unaccompanied by an adult. Without previous library experience, they may be wondering if they should be there and they should be introduced to the range of materials and services available without having to ask for assistance. It may be possible to arrange for them to work with buddies who are already familiar with how the library works, and who can answer some of the basic questions.

■ Book Selection

When asked about book selection, Alma Flor Ada stated, "Children have the right to the familiar and the non-familiar . . . . Their horizons need to be expanded." (Ada 1998). If American children were limited to books written in the United States, they would not have Peter Rabbit, Pippi Longstocking, or Winnie-the-Pooh. Therefore, as mentioned in Chapter 2, acquisition of Spanish-language materials need not be limited to those published in a particular country, or even in the Americas. Good literature touches the reader, broadens the reader's horizon, validates experiences and invites reflection (Ada 1990, 3); meaningful stories come from human experience, raise universal issues, speak to readers across cultures, and offer the potential for multiple interpretations (Hudelson et al. 1994).

At the same time, it is important for students to see illustrations of people who look like and have similar value systems as themselves in the books they read, not just white, middle-class *Leave-It-To-Beaver* Americans. And, the white, middle-class kids need to realize that the realities of other ethnic groups are just as valid as their own and may be more similar than they think. Just as the shelves of grocery stores reflect the needs of their communities, so should the shelves of a library (Sykes 1990, 12).

Selection Criteria

It may not be possible for librarians who know little Spanish to thoroughly analyze materials for selection, especially in the absence of critical reviews, but guidelines developed for evaluating children's books are applicable to materials for all age levels. The following have been adapted from Schon (1995), Salabiye (1990), Allen (1993), and the Council on Interracial Books (n.d.):

1. Are the settings accurate? Do the flora and fauna accurately represent the locale? Do the characters live in a variety of urban and rural settings and come from a variety of socioeconomic levels?

2. Do the author and illustrator have knowledgeable perspectives of the cultures, settings, and circumstances about which they are writing/illustrating?

3. Are there negative stereotypes or distortions of Latino culture? Are the characters portrayed as poverty-stricken, lazy, dirty, or having other negative qualities? Are the women only homemakers in traditional dresses with their hair in buns or braids? Look for other subtle misrepresentations or stereotypes of all ethnic groups mentioned, not just Latinos.

4. Is this quality literature with entertaining plots and characters, attractive illustrations, and Latino/a heroes/heroines who solve their own problems?

5. Are the positive, unique qualities of the culture presented appropriately as opposed to showing happy, carefree peasants in oppressive or demeaning circumstances?

6. Is the book visually attractive with quality binding?

7. For nonfiction, compare the original copyright date with the date of translations (if applicable). Materials printed in Latin America may not be updated as often as we would like, so the information could be outdated.

8. Was the translation done by a native speaker? Is the translator an author in his or her own right—someone who can appreciate what it takes to write an appealing book?

As with younger students, bilingual and semibilingual books have a place among middle grade students. Familiar Spanish words and phrases plus strong illustrations can help Spanish-dominant children feel more comfortable about their ability to understand text that is primarily in English. However, the Spanish words do need to be used correctly within proper context, not just thrown in haphazardly for effect. At the same time, the more Spanish an English-speaker is exposed to and helped to understand, the more empathy the English-speaker should have for a Spanish-speaking classmate or friend (Agosto 1997).

An article in the *Journal of Adolescent & Adult Literacy* (Cassady 1998) recommends using wordless books with reluctant or struggling readers of all ages for language and vocabulary development in either the first or second language. Students can read their own stories into a tape recorder while looking at the illustrations. The text can then be typed out so the student can read the story over and over, helping reinforce the connection between written and spoken language. If appropriate, these same books and cassette tapes could also be used with younger, beginning, or pre-emergent readers.

Students of all ethnic backgrounds need the same easy access to age-appropriate information. Illustration-rich books such as those published by Dorling Kindersley, in either or both languages, would be useful in graphically conveying subject-related content and concepts, and can help LEP students understand how previous learning connects to present learning. Books in English published with a simplified vocabulary for younger children can be used effectively if they do not appear too juvenile.

Types of Materials

The types of Spanish-language books mentioned as being especially good for this age group include (Mestre and Nieto 1996, 30; Ramirez and Dowd 1997):

Audiocassettes (music and spoken)

Beginning reference books such as almanacs and atlases

Biographies of historical, literary, and cultural figures

Children's encyclopedia(s)

Comic books, games, and puzzles

Contemporary issues such as immigration, bilingualism, migrant labor, prejudice/discrimination, intercultural marriage, and intercultural adoption, in nonfiction and fiction

Dictionaries: Spanish-only, Spanish/English

ESL for children

Higher education, career opportunities

Hispanic, Latin American, and indigenous folklore, legends, mythology, and art

Historical accounts reflecting perspectives of the particular cultures/peoples discussed

How-to, hobby books in English and Spanish (with clear diagrams and illustrations)

Magazines

Native Spanish-language children's authors (As you begin to collect titles listed in standard selection tools [listed in Appendix A], you will become familiar with the names of important Latino authors.)

Picture books

Poetry

Positive contemporary Hispanic/Latino role models

Same subject areas as in English

Sports (Find out which are most popular with your patrons.)

Supplemental materials for school curriculum

Translations of classics or favorites that others are reading in English

Videocassettes (to supplement curriculum and to entertain)

Wordless books

World Cultures

Can I Find What I Need?

To ensure that information is always available for school assignments, the Riverside (Calif.) Public Library places some of the popular books in Reference (ones that would not ordinarily be classified as Reference) and also creates pamphlet files and loose-leaf notebooks from books that have fallen apart and are beyond repair. They also often purchase several copies of a few good Spanish titles rather than one copy of several titles (Struthers 1998).

New materials should be purchased on a regular basis, just as materials are purchased for other areas of the collection. Latino children want to feel that their book and reading needs have just as high a priority as the needs of every other language group in the community, and it is always fun to be the first to turn the pages of a new book. Many libraries try to use a percentage of their budget for Spanish-language materials that equates to the percentage of Spanish-speakers in the population served, although for most it is a goal not yet met. In a school setting, in particular, it helps to preview as many titles as possible so you can get assistance from others such as bilingual teachers and aides.

Library Skills

Teaching library skills may be tricky if the library staff does not speak Spanish, but several people emphasized that "good enough" (not perfect) Spanish can go a long way to show children you are making a sincere effort to help them. Make learning library terminology a two-way street—you learn the Spanish from them at the same time you teach them English. If working with a group of mixed-language students, the classroom teacher may be able to help with on-the-spot translations. Having reference tools in Spanish would definitely help students in learning such skills as: alphabetization—use of dictionary; using an encyclopedia, almanac, or atlas; and note-taking, or writing a research paper. Once the specific skills are learned, they should be easily transferable between languages.

Jean Parry (1999), School District Librarian for Lake County School District in Leadville, Colorado describes an incident that happened to her:

> Our sixth grade social studies teacher and I did an atlas-almanac-encyclopedia unit where I described an imaginary journey. I would start out in the town where I teach and take them to the town where I grew up, and all of this was described both by coordinates—latitude and longitude—and then also with an historical fact, or something that made that place unique. We were doing OK explaining this in English and Spanish but the Spanish-speaking students just didn't seem real happy until we placed a Spanish language almanac, a Spanish language encyclopedia and a Spanish language atlas in front of each of them. And their eyes lit up, because they realized, for the first time perhaps, that this school and these teachers were prepared for them, and wanted them to be an active part of the classroom activities, just as much so as the students who spoke English.

■ Program Ideas

There are any number of great programming ideas that can be used to promote reading, most of which can be used with younger and older students. Many of the ideas are from school settings but could be easily adapted by public libraries for after-school or summer-reading programs. Most of the ideas could be used with children of any nationality, but the following ideas seem especially appropriate for use with Spanish-speakers and their families. As with any library program, much of the success will depend on the person in charge and whether that person can readily relate to the intended audience.

"Read Across America Day"

"Read Across America Day" (March 2), in conjunction with Dr. Seuss's birthday, is a good opportunity to invite community members into libraries to read. Be sure to have some of the Spanish versions of Dr. Seuss's books in the library. Look beyond your usual pool of readers to find other people who might be able to read or tell stories in Spanish: custodians, bus drivers, secretaries, cafeteria workers, and high school sports stars in addition to major and minor league sports players and local television and radio personalities.

One public library invited parents in for Family Reading Night and then the local school continued with Reading Night the first Monday of the month for the rest of the school year. A school in Portland, Oregon, offered Donuts for Dads and Muffins for Moms for parents who stopped in before school to read with students. How about changing the name to *Pancitos para Papá* and *Merienda para Mamá?* Libraries in New Mexico and Texas have used a musical bookwalk (a variation of a cakewalk) where children paraded or danced along a marked route, and those landing on particular spaces when the music stopped won prizes (books, of course).

These ideas and others can be found at the web site: http://www.nea.org/readacross/.

National Library Week

The Fort Lupton (Colo.) schools and public library hold a Reading Celebration in April for National Library Week. This program was held after school from 4 to 7 PM, and as many as 250 students sat spread out on blankets on the school lawn to read to an additional 300 family members. Students reading three books (from home or the library) have their names entered into a drawing for 10 major door prizes. All participating students receive coupons for free pizza and ice-cream cones from local restaurants, and siblings who listen to stories get a coupon for one or the other. Depending on the budget available to the individual library, pizza or finger foods can be served (Martinez 1998).

Día de los Niños: Día de los Libros

Because *Día de los Niños* (Children's Day) is celebrated in Mexico on April 30, author Pat Mora has been instrumental in appropriating that day to also celebrate *Día de los Libros* (Book Day), a day to recognize the benefits of bilingual literacy. Young people could be involved (perhaps a cooperative effort with Spanish- and English-speakers) in creating bilingual posters, banners, murals, and bookmarks to be placed around the school and community to advertise the event. This would be an appropriate time to involve families in writing or audio-taping family or neighborhood stories, or making collections of traditional songs, recipes, sayings, and games (*Día de los Niños,* 32). Going a step further, after writing out instructions to a game, a group of children could be videotaped playing the game.

In Santa Fe, New Mexico, the Museum of International Folk Art joined with the local school district and public library and hosted a bilingual family afternoon featuring bookmaking activities as well as reading by children and authors. Bookmaking offers unlimited possibilities for creativity as children brainstorm the different materials they could use, traditional (paper, cloth) and offbeat (refrigerator boxes, handmade paper, birch bark, etc.). Other types of museums also have exhibits highlighting accomplishments of Latinos and could be tapped for cooperative programs.

Additional ideas for *Día de los Niños: Día de los Libros* can be found at the Texas State Library Web site: http://www.tsl.state.tx.us/ld/projects/ninos/title/contents.htm.

Children's Book Week

Children's Book Week is celebrated in November and might be a good time to invite local or well-known authors in to read stories. Hold a writing workshop with the author and have students and teachers write their own Spanish, English and/or bilingual book(s). Make copies of the books so children can take them home as well as place them in the library, medical center, hospital, or health department for others to read. With just a little extra effort the books could be laminated so they are more durable. Children could also be videotaped reading some of their favorite books or telling favorite stories.

The *Herald Democrat*, a weekly newspaper in Leadville, Colorado periodically publishes short pieces in English and Spanish that elementary school students have written in class. The thrill of being "published" is a great motivator for the kids. Do not overlook the school's newspaper or Web site as other places to publish students' works.

Any Time of the Year

We librarians cannot imagine anything better than curling up with a good book and reading all day, but students may not have experienced that joy. Teachers in Eastern Canada faced the dilemma of trying to turn Inuit students onto reading in their native language, Inuktitut (which has more of an oral than a written tradition) and English. Rising to the challenge, they adopted the DEAR (Drop Everything And Read) model. At scheduled and unannounced times during the day (similar to a fire drill), everyone in the school was to stop what they were doing, go to unconventional, designated places and read. Teachers read in the hallway, boys in the girls' bathroom, and custodians in the school office. At one point during the long winter months, they fashioned a large bed of gym mats, quilts, and pillows outside the office, and selected students got to read in bed—very popular with the students (Cumming 1997).

The San Antonio Public Library develops bicultural programming packets to encompass the whole year, with programs about all the ethnic groups in their city. Several libraries could get together and share the responsibility for developing such packets, with all participants receiving copies of the final results. That way several libraries benefit from expertise that might not be available to them directly (Treviño 1999). With variations, the same themes are presented in programs for preschoolers at the public library as well as in school library programs for older students.

On a similar line, librarians could develop theme/resource packets to accompany units that are regularly taught by classroom teachers. The packets would emphasize graphic and hands-on material or exercises especially for students of limited English ability, and could be used in the classroom or library. Bibliographies of Spanish language books, magazines, videos, Web sites, or encyclopedia articles on the subject could also be included.

One librarian in Minnesota has hosted book-buying sprees for students and staff to local bookstores. If you have a little extra money and a group of Spanish-speakers you really want to hook into using the library and/or people whose opinions you especially value and wish to reward (perhaps student aides), a book-buying spree might be a good way to involve that group of students in improving the library's Spanish-language collection.

If a local bookstore or publisher features Hispanic authors during promotional tours for those authors' works, arrange for these authors to visit the school and public libraries while they are in town.

A school librarian in Arkansas purchased a varied collection of such topics as cookbooks, drawing books, how-tos, paper folding, cheerleading, and string games. As part of a library period she put out scrap paper, pencils, and other supplies so that, as the students silently read the new books, they could also try out some of the ideas they found (Wallace 1998). This would be a great hands-on way for English-learners to become comfortable using books for recreational reading and learning other fun activities. It would also be good for introducing all students to traditional arts and crafts from the various ethnic groups represented in the community.

Find as many ways as possible to put books into students' hands. In cooperation with the public library, hold book fairs or book swaps on the same days or nights as Parent/Teacher Conferences. Even if families cannot afford to buy books, arrange for each child to go home with at least one new book.

Have parents help create "grandmother trunks" with items representing different ethnic groups: clothing, art or craft items, pictures, magazine articles, and books. If items are especially unusual, be sure to include an explanation of their significance. This could be part of or in addition to ethnic learning centers (Beilke and Sciara 1986, 38–39).

During the year, use some or all of the following to create displays: picture postcards, stamps, paper money, traditional decorations, and posters from travel agencies or national tourism agencies. Posters of scenic or historic areas of Latin American countries should be of interest to everyone, but try to avoid pictures of beaches with bronzed, bikini-clad bodies—not a scene with which everyone can relate, and often more a reflection of the tourist industry than of actual residents. When you or friends are on vacation, pick up pictures, folk art, and other decorations from the countries you visit. Use them on a regular basis to make the library a friendly place, not just for special occasions.

Internet

The Internet opens up many possibilities for Spanish-speakers to find information to meet their needs. Bookmark Web sites that are particularly good sources of information so they are readily available. See Chapter 7 for a list of possible URLs.

MECHA (Migrant Education Consortium for Higher Achievement) is a project being developed by Miami-Dade County Public Schools and Barry University to help improve the educational success of migrant children. Families of selected students receive a Web TV unit which they take with them as they travel. An individualized learning plan is developed for each student, and a MECHA teacher monitors the students' progress as well as designs lessons that use Internet resources. If this project proves successful and is implemented elsewhere, librarians may be challenged to provide services to this kind of mobile clientele, as well as those who live just around the corner (Greenleaf et al. 1999).

Although Orillas (officially: *De Orilla a Orilla*, From Shore to Shore) was developed in the mid-1980s as a computer-based global learning network to cultivate multicultural understanding among students in bilingual settings, the concept could be used in libraries for a long-term enrichment activity. Using the medium of e-mail over the Internet, students could share messages with a group of peers in another part of the United States or in another country, in Spanish and/or English. For more information about the project contact: Dr. Dennis Sayers, NYU School of Education, New York, NY 10003.

A similar project, I*EARN (International Education and Resource Network), began in 1988 to help classrooms of students use available technology to interact internationally and begin to deal with pressing global issues. Some facility with other languages may be needed depending on the part of the world from which the cooperating classroom comes (J. Brown 1999, 40). Further information can be obtained from: I*EARN, 475 Riverside Dr., Room 540, New York, NY 10115; 212-870-2693; http://www.iearn.org.

Book Clubs

When you have copies of the same popular book(s) in English and Spanish, hold a bilingual book club. The club could also serve as conversation practice, for students learning English as well as those learning Spanish. Jean Parry described a version of this (1999):

> In our elementary school we do lots of buddy reading where two children both read the same book. So, we have lots of books for English-speaking students that want to buddy read and we have multiple copies of books in Spanish for Spanish-speaking students that want to buddy read with each other, but it dawned on me: Now wait a minute, what happens if I have a Spanish-speaking student and an English-speaking student who want to buddy read? And so we began buying lots of bilingual books, plus books in English and Spanish—the same title—so that we didn't create an artificial barrier based on language between two children who might otherwise become friends. The bilingual books took off and we often noticed a

Spanish-speaking student reading in Spanish and then an English-speaking student reading the same passage in English. And also it is typical that the Spanish version and the English version of the same book will be checked out at the same time by two friends who plan to read together.

Homework Help

Homework Help programs are needed in situations where children are struggling with their schoolwork, and are perhaps unable to receive the help they need at home. Schools, libraries, and other community agencies have set up after-school and telephone programs to assist with homework issues. Bilingual aides would be essential in this case so they can switch between languages as needed.

Budding Authors

There are any number of activities that can encourage students to write their own works, in either or both languages. Let students take an instant camera and take pictures around town or school, and then write a story based on the resulting photographs. Have them make up captions for amusing photos from newspapers or magazines. They can write their own real or pretend biographies; create comics; write plays for people actors or for puppets (Lindfors 1989, 46–49).

Because Mexico has a long history of public art in the form of murals, have Latino students illustrate stories they have written with murals drawn on long sheets of newsprint in the form of murals, or have them create the murals first and then write the stories. This idea could easily be combined with studies in any number of subject areas such as art, social studies, or folk literature (Mestre and Nieto 1996, 33). For further ideas see some of Diego Rivera's murals at: http://www.diegorivera.com.

With a little imagination there are out-of-date machines that could be used by students in their creative endeavors: overhead projectors, slide projectors, filmstrip projectors, and so forth. Christine Igoa made extensive use of filmstrips to have her students write and illustrate their own stories (Brown, K. 1993; Igoa 1995). As students gain more and more computer literacy, there are also programs that allow them to write text and create pictures, or scan in photographs. Even ancient computers, if still functional, have poster- and greeting card-making software with graphics that could be used for this purpose.

Youngsters can participate in choral reading or Readers' Theater. With a class of English- and Spanish-speakers, you could use the same book in both languages and have the story read alternately in both languages. Have the kids switch parts: the English-speakers read the Spanish and vice versa.

Cooperative Efforts

Cooperative programming efforts are just as important with this middle-grade age group as with any other. Offer the library's meeting room or other resources to youth organizations in the community: Boy and Girl Scouts, 4-H, or other such organizations. From my own work with the Girl Scouts, I know the organization is exploring creative avenues for meeting the needs of girls and young women whom they have not traditionally served.

Mexican Opportunities

The Mexican Government offers programs for American teachers working with Mexican students including Teacher Exchanges and immersion courses for bilingual teachers as well as other summer classes offered at Mexican universities. Youth organizations interested in developing summer recreational activities can request that a Mexican physical education or recreation teacher come into the community to direct those efforts for five weeks. The Mexican National Commission of Sport covers the cost of transportation to the United States; the sponsoring organization basically needs to provide for housing, food, medical insurance, and other minimal expenses for the Mexican teacher during that teacher's stay. For more information contact the nearest Mexican consulate or cultural institute.

■ Periodicals

Addresses of Distributors

C.D.S., Subscriptions Dept.
    PO Box 37253
    Boone, IA 50037

Continental Book Company
    625 E. 70th Ave. #5
    Denver, CO 80229

    80-00 Cooper Ave. #29
    Glendale, NY

EBSCO, International Headquarters
    PO Box 11943
    Birmingham, AL 35201-1943

Latin American Periodicals
    2555 N. Coyote Dr., Suite 109
    Tucson, AZ 85745

Spanish Publications Inc.
    PO Box 742149
    Houston, TX 77274-2149

Spanish Periodicals & Book Sales
    10100 NW 25th St.
    Miami, FL 33172
    http://www.spanishperiodical.com

Periodical Titles

Mary Glasgow Magazines

Scholastic, Inc.
    PO Box 3710
    Jefferson City, MO 65102-3710
    Also available through EBSCO.

> Although designed for students of Spanish as a second language, the more advanced levels of these colorful eight-page magazines could also serve students for whom Spanish is the first language. Titles are: Level 1: *¿Qué Tal?*; Level 2: *Ahora*; Level 3: *El Sol*; Advanced: *Hoy Día.* An impressive range of topics was covered in the four issues reviewed.

MEP, Midwest European Publications, Inc.

Subscription Dept.
    915 Foster St.
    Evanston, IL 60201-3199
    http://www.mep-eli.com

> Although geared for students of Spanish rather than native speakers, MEP does have four publications: *¡Vamos!* (Beginning level); *Muchachos* (Intermediate); *Chicos* (Advanced beginner); and *Todos Amigos* (Intermediate-Advanced). The colorful magazines have short blurbs about people and topics of interest to teens, but are written in a form of Spanish more common in Spain than in Latin America.

La Nueva Edad de Oro: Revista Para los Niños de América

Fundación José Martí
    3400 Coral Way, Suite 602
    Miami, FL 33145

Magazine with a variety of articles (cooking, arts and crafts, guessing games); submissions by readers encouraged. A few of the reading activities do seem to require reference back to stories in the original *La Edad de Oro* by José Martí.

Scholastic Classroom Magazines

Scholastic News en Español
P.O. Box 3710
Jefferson City, MO 65102-3710
Distributed by: EBSCO
http://www.scholastic.com

Geared for use in a classroom setting, the three levels (Grades 1–3) of *Scholastic News en Español*, published weekly during the school year, could also be used as supplemental material in a school library, especially where there was no bilingual or Spanish-language instruction. Teachers ordering 10 or more copies receive a free Teacher's Guide.

Tú

Distributors: Latin American Periodicals; EBSCO; Continental Book Co.; Subscription: C.D.S.

A monthly magazine for younger teens dealing with the subjects teens are interested in: boy/girl relationships, fashion, beauty, music, and stars of the entertainment world.

Zoobooks: En Español

Wildlife Education, Ltd.
12233 Thatcher Ct.
Poway, CA 92064-6880
Distributed by EBSCO

The same as the English magazine, with each issue featuring a specific animal.

■ Other Resources

Education Publications Center
P.O. Box 1398
Jessup, MD 20794-1398
http://www.ed.gov/offices/OIIA/spanishresources/edpubs.html

Offers the following publications to assist parents in helping children with schoolwork:

- *Cómo Ayudar a Sus Hijos a Aprender Ciencia* (How to Help Your Child Learn Science)
- *Cómo Ayudar a Sus Hijos a Aprender Matemáticas* (. . . Math)
- *Cómo Ayudarle a Su Hijo con la Tarea Escolar* (. . . with Homework
- *¡Juguemos a las Matemáticas!* (Let's Play with Math)
- *¡Leamos!* (Let's Read)
- *Cómo Ayudar a Su Hijo a Aprender a Leer* (. . . Learn to Read)

Scholastic Spanish/English Book Club/*Scholastic Club de Lectura* and Scholastic Book Fairs: http://www.scholastic.com
P. O. Box 7500
Jefferson City, MO 65102-7500
1-800-724-6527

Low-cost books for pre-kindergarten to grade five that can be purchased for home or classroom use. Selections in English and Spanish are available.

Reading is Fundamental, Inc. (RIF)
600 Maryland Ave., SW, Suite 600
Smithsonian Institution, Washington, D.C. 20024

See program description in Chapter 3.

Project WILD: http://www.projectwild.org/wildnews.html#Spanish
707 Conservation Lane, Suite 305
Gaithersburg, MD 20878
301-527-8900

In response to the demand for Spanish-language materials, Project WILD is translating a collection of its environmental education activities.

Bilingual Posters and Bookmarks

Upstart
W5527 Highway 106, P. O. Box 800
Fort Atkinson, WI 53538-0800
1-800-448-4887

Offers a selection of bilingual and/or multicultural posters, bookmarks, and banners. Many of the whimsical stickers and patches have no words, so could be used with youngsters of any language background.

ALA Graphics

> American Library Association
> 155 N. Wacker Dr.
> Chicago, IL 60606
> 1-800-545-2433

> > ALA offers bilingual "Lea/Read" and literacy posters, as well as infant clothing for the "Born to Read" campaign.

Hispanic Heritage Editions: http://www.chicanoartist.com

> P.O. Box 944
> Bernalillo, NM 87004
> 505-771-3030

> > Some of the publishers and distributors listed in Appendix C also carry these kinds of materials.

■ Works Cited

Ada, Alma Flor. *A Magical Encounter: Spanish-Language Children's Literature in the Classroom.* Compton, Calif.: Santillana, 1990.

———. Interview with author, Denver, Colo., 24 April 1998.

Agosto, Denise. "Bilingual Picture Books: Libros Para Todos," *School Library Journal* (Aug. 1997): 38–39.

Allen, Adela Artola, editor. *Library Services for Hispanic Children: A Guide for Public and School Librarians.* Phoenix: Oryx Press, 1987.

———. "The School Library Media Center and the Promotion of Literature for Hispanic Children." *Library Trends* (Winter 1993): 437–455.

Beilke, Patricia F. and Frank J. Sciara. *Selecting Materials for and about Hispanic and East Asian Children and Young People.* Hamden, Conn.: Library Professional Publications, 1986.

Brown, Justine K. "Indigenous Connections through I*EARN." *Converge* (April 1999): 40–42.

Brown, Kristin. Balancing the Tools of Technology with Our Own Humanity: The Use of Technology in Building Partnerships and Communities. In *The Power of Two Languages: Literacy and Biliteracy for Spanish-Speaking Students*, edited by Josefina Villamil Tinajero and Alma Flor Ada. New York: Macmillan McGraw-Hill School Publishing, 1993.

Cassady, Judith K. "Wordless Books: No-Risk Tools for Inclusive Middle-Grade Classrooms," *Journal of Adolescent & Adult Literacy* (March 1998): 428—432.

Council on Interracial Books for Children. *10 Quick Ways to Analyze Children's Books for Racism and Sexism.* (n.d.). [Online] Available: http://www.birchlane.davis.ca.us/library/10quick.htm (Accessed May 14, 1998).

Cumming, Peter. "Drop Everything and Read All Over: Literacy and Loving It," *The Horn Book Magazine* (Nov.-Dec. 1997): 714–717.

Cummins, Jim. " Beyond Adversarial Discourse: Searching for Common Ground in the Education of Bilingual Students." Paper presented at Annual International Bilingual/Multicultural Education Conference of National Association for Bilingual Education, Denver, Colo., 28 Jan. 1999.

———. *Empowering Minority Students.* Sacramento, Calif.: California Association for Bilingual Education, 1989.

"Día de los Niños: Día de los Libros." *REFORMA Newsletter* 17 (Summer 1998): 32.

Greenleaf, Janie et al. *Project MECHA: Distance Learning Linking Migrant Learning.* Presentation given at Annual International Bilingual/Multicultural Education Conference, National Association of Bilingual Education, 28 Jan. 1999, Denver, Colo.

Hudelson, Sarah et al. "Chasing Windmills: Confronting the Obstacles to Literature-Based Programs in Spanish," *Language Arts* (March 1994): 164–171.

Igoa, Cristina. *The Inner World of the Immigrant Child.* New York: St. Martin's Press, 1995.

Lindfors, Judith Wells. The Classroom: A Good Environment. In *When They Don't All Speak English: Integrating the ESL Student into the Regular Classroom,* edited by Pat Rigg and Virginia G. Allen. Urbana, Ill.: National Council of Teachers of English, 1989.

Martinez, Rosalie. Personal interview with author, Ft. Lupton, Colo., 18 May 1998.

McQuillan, Jeff and Lucy Tse. "Child Language Brokering in Linguistic Minority Communities: Effects on Cultural Interaction, Cognition, and Literacy," *Language and Education* 9 no. 3 (1995): 195–215.

Mestre, Lori S. and Sonia Nieto. "Puerto Rican Children's Literature and Culture in the Public Library," *MultiCultural Review* (June 1996): 26–39.

Mora, Pat. "Día de los Niños: Día de los Libros: Bilingual Literacy Day," *United States Board on Books for Young People, Inc. Newsletter* (Spring 1998): 15–18.

National Education Association. *NEA: Read Across America - Event Ideas.* (n.d.) [Online]. Available: http://www.nea.org/readacross/ideas.html (Accessed Dec. 31, 1998).

Parry, Jean. Conversation with author, Leadville, Colo., 16 March 1999.

Ramirez, Melva and Frances Smardo Dowd. "Another Look at the Portrayal of Mexican-American Females in Realistic Picture Books: A Content Analysis, 1990-1997," *MultiCultural Review* (December 1997): 20–27+.

Salabiye, Velma. Selection of Materials for Culturally Diverse Communities. In *Developing Library Collections for California's Emerging Majority: A Manual of Resources for Ethnic Collection Development*, edited by Katharine Scarborough. Berkeley, Calif.: University of California, Berkeley School of Library and Information Studies, 1990.

Schon, Isabel. "Spanish-Language Books for Young Readers - Great Expectations, Disappointing Realities," *Booklist* (1 Oct. 1995): 318–319.

Sosa, Alicia. *Thorough and Fair: Creating Routes to Success for Mexican-American Students.* Charleston, W.V.: ERIC Clearinghouse on Rural Education and Small Schools, 1993.

Struthers, Sue. Telephone interview, 10 Nov. 1998.

Sykes, Vivian. Advocacy for Ethnic Collection Development. In *Developing Library Collections for California's Emerging Majority: A Manual of Resources for Ethnic Collection Development*, edited by Katharine Scarborough. Berkeley, Calif.: University of California, Berkeley School of Library and Information Studies, 1990.

Texas State Library. *Día de los Niños: Día de los Libros.* (n.d.) [Online]. Available: http://www.tsl.state.tx.us/id/projects/ninos/contents.htm (Accessed April 10, 1998).

Treviño, Rose. Telephone interview, 29 March 1999.

Tse, Lucy. "When an ESL Adult Becomes a Reader," *Reading Horizons* 37 no.1(1996): 16-29.

Wallace, Suby. "I've Had the Best Week." In LM_NET [Online listserv, accessed Oct. 20, 1998]; available from *LM_NET@listserv.syr.edu.*

Chapter 5

The Teenage Years

■ Basic Education

The teen years are often hard on all teens as they test their own limits, as well as society's in the process of becoming independent adults. However, immigrant teens, who are struggling to adapt to a new culture and language at the same time, have an even more difficult adjustment.

We hope those teens who arrived in the United States as grade schoolers or younger have made a successful transition to the American educational system, although their academic skill levels in English may still lag behind those of most of their nonimmigrant classmates. Those who have arrived more recently are having to adjust to different pedagogical systems with emphases on skills to which they may not have been introduced previously. Participating in class discussions, changing classes at the sound of a bell, and storing personal items in a locker may all be new concepts. Additional stressors may result from transience, irregular legal status, or poor literacy skills in the first language. Furthermore, at this time of life when acceptance by peers and that special someone takes on great importance, immigrant teens may find that role expectations in our society are different from those to which they have been accustomed. Because the social cliques may have been long established, teens may not feel they fit anywhere.

These young people are faced with a small window in which to complete their basic education—master the basics of English and catch up on all the other subject areas they are expected to know by high school graduation. Very likely they will also need help in learning how to learn in ways U.S. educators expect.

For many, catching up may seem like an impossible task, and as statistics show, the 30 percent dropout rate by Hispanic teens is greater than for any other ethnic group. These students need to believe there is hope of graduating and of securing employment that offers opportunities beyond manual labor (Anstrom 1998, 4; Headden 1998; Minicucci and Olsen 1992, 3–6). It will take the combined efforts of teens, their families, the community, and businesses to see that they do not take the "easy" route of dropping out (LARASA June 1998).

Many of these teens may not have family members who have completed 12 years of basic education. In Mexico, for example, nine years are considered to be the standard, although not everyone completes even that much. Even though parents and other family members may be ill at ease visiting a high school because of their own lack of education, they should still be encouraged to participate in school functions and shown that they do have valuable life lessons to pass on to their sons and daughters. Studies have shown there is a strong correlation between parental involvement and student achievement, so the longer parents stay connected, the better (Navarrette 1996). If ESL and parenting of teenager classes are not available elsewhere in the community, those could be valuable services to provide to adults in the evenings when the high school library is otherwise unoccupied. A lending library especially for adults could help extend a welcome in a concrete way.

There is often a misperception that ESL teachers can prepare LEP high school students for the regular classroom in a short period of time. As was shown earlier, second-language acquisition is not a quick, easy process, and by this age students may be especially self-conscious about attempting to speak the new language for fear of making embarrassing mistakes. Secondary teachers of content areas may not be trained to work with LEP students, however, and the act of changing classes and teachers several times a day means students do not develop close relationships with any teachers. On the other hand, those who do have a good command of English may resist using Spanish and therefore helping struggling peers because they may not feel it is "cool" to be bilingual.

High school library staff may have an advantage in relating to these teens if the staff can be seen as advocates in the learning process. If students can visit the library before and after school and during study halls or other free periods, there is greater opportunity for the library staff to get to know them and make them feel welcome, pointing out resources that will be helpful or sometimes just lending a friendly ear. As you get to know them, recruit some of these students as library aides. Some schools require students to complete internships or periods of volunteer work, so library service might qualify to fulfill this requirement.

Melvina Azar Dame (1994) developed strategies in her high school library to help LEP students avoid fear of the unfamiliar. Her initial steps included giving these students a special library orientation when no other classes were present, including hands-on experience using the photocopier, computers, and other machines. Later, when students returned to work on other assignments, they were instructed to go to Dame for personal assistance. With this individualized approach the young people found the library a friendly, welcoming place. A similar orientation to the public library, perhaps as part of a class, could show students what is available there.

In addition to her efforts at library skills instruction for Spanish-speaking students, Dame initiated a Spanish/English literacy activity where Anglo students of Spanish IV interacted orally with native speakers who were also high school students. Besides the chance to practice conversation in the two languages, the sessions gave students opportunities to learn about each other's cultures and ultimately to become friends. Dame found that initially when a misunderstanding about cultural differences arose or Anglo students made invalid assumptions, the Latinos needed to be encouraged and empowered to recognize the misperceptions and offer explanations that might bring clearer understanding.

Ideally, all students will be given an opportunity to study and appreciate works by authors of color, not just those students studying other languages. If this is not an area of expertise of the literature instructor, the library/media specialist could suggest possible titles, team-teach with the instructor, or personally teach the class.

Because in many Latin American countries the public library is seen as a quiet place to get together with friends to study, U.S. public libraries could take advantage of that perception to attract teens, although teenagers in general are inclined to be the most underserved library population. Once in the door, however, the young people need to be shown, over time, that the library is more than just a fancy study hall, and allowed and encouraged to use the full range of library services to their benefit. Sympathetic staff members can assist them in finding library resources that meet their needs—for homework and life in general. Because their free time is often limited by jobs and other family responsibilities, library services need to be effective and efficient (Sanchez et al. 1989, 18).

■ Leisure Activities

Many people of lower socioeconomic status, including teens, have not had the luxury of discovering reading as a pleasurable leisure-time activity. By providing a wide range of reading materials in English and Spanish, and the time and encouragement to participate in free voluntary reading, libraries can help teens improve not only reading, but also vocabulary, grammar, and writing skills. Krashen (1998, 1–16) argues that free voluntary reading (no strings attached) may be more beneficial for language acquisition and literacy development than direct instruction. The reading material need not directly support the school's curriculum—sports, automotive or movie star magazines, romance novels, or comic books—just about anything that makes reading appealing to a population who might need to be convinced.

Literature-based literacy programs in either the first or second language, depending on students' needs, can make use of light fiction such as children's books, adolescent fiction, and newspapers and magazines. Such series as *Sweet*

Valley High have proven successful even with adults because these books give a narrow reading experience: all titles in the series have recurring context, vocabulary, and characters, but are interesting and allow students to build reading skills as they progress (McQuillan and Rodrigo 1998, 209–224).

A survey done at the Oakland (Calif.) Public Library about a decade ago sought to determine the interests and favorite free time activities of teen respondents, over 60 percent of who were Hispanic. The number one activity was listening to the radio, followed by watching television, participating in sports, and talking on the telephone. Reading came in at a dismal fifth place (Sanchez et al. 1989, 33). A more recent survey done by Nielsen Media Research indicates that the top Spanish-language television shows for teens in the United States are *novelas* (soap opera-type shows), but that sitcoms and action series are also popular. When it comes to individual celebrities, Hispanic teens prefer black male athletes followed by Hispanic male and female musicians and white actors. Although some of the popularity of these figures may be due to the hype of the media, it does give some indication of what appeals to these teens (Mendosa 1998).

■ Marketing to Latino Teens

In trying to serve Latino teens as well as adults, it is critical, once you have a community of Spanish-speakers and have begun to establish rapport, to identify teens who could serve on a library advisory council to help provide ideas, act as word-of-mouth advertising agencies, and invite friends to come along to the great programs at the library. Successful programs most often result from community needs assessments (see Alire and Archibeque), or are initiated by other community entities with the library as a partner (Sanchez et al. 1989, 22).

Teens who have dropped out of school may be one of the more difficult populations to reach because they have given up on education and may see libraries as an extension of the failure-filled school environment. Therefore, taking library services in through the back door of another agency may be one of the best ways to show what the library has to offer pertaining to recreation and real life. Relevant programs could reach teens in programs for pregnant, unwed mothers, for drug and alcohol abuse, and through GED classes.

If your community has juvenile detention centers or facilities for the mentally, emotionally, or physically disabled, Latino young people may be disproportionately represented and may benefit from having Spanish-language or bilingual library services taken to them (Sanchez et al. 1989, 16). In my own community college setting, I am often well aware of the young people who have had brushes with the law or who are having trouble with classes because they have not taken study seriously. As long as they behave reasonably well in the library, I can ignore those other problems and try to connect with the neat personalities they have hidden within them.

To market to the majority of teens who are not in trouble or in need of specialized medical or counseling services, advertise the library in places where teens congregate such as malls, music stores, parks, restaurants and, as indicated previously, on local television and radio stations. Although having food or drink in or near the library is a sometimes touchy subject, some libraries have found that edibles can be a draw for always-hungry teens.

■ Young-Adult Literature – ¿Sí O No?

The need for young-adult literature is just now beginning to be recognized in Latin American countries. In traditional thought, young people remained children until age 15, at which time they became adults, therefore no need was seen for any transitional literature (Rodriguez 1995). *Quinceañera* celebrations, held by many Latino families as sort of "coming out" parties for their 15-year-old daughters, are rites of passage from childhood to adulthood.

According to author Pat Mora (1998), the supply of Spanish-language books for teens in the United States is market-driven and publishers are given the message that there is no need for such material. Librarians who scrounge far and wide for suitable teenage materials should give them a different message.

Popular Topics

The following are book subjects about which Spanish-speaking teens may especially want or need to read, but be sure to consult with them also for their suggestions (Sanchez et al. 1989, 34–35):

AIDS (*SIDA* in Spanish) and other STDs

Audiotapes and videotapes

Automobiles including low-riders

Authors of color (for Latinos and non-Latinos)

Body art including tattooing and piercing

College and career choices

Computers and World Wide Web/Internet

Contemporary issues such as immigration, bilingualism, migrant labor, prejudice/discrimination, intercultural marriage, and adoption, in non-fiction and fiction

Date rape

Dictionaries—Spanish and Spanish/English

Drinking and driving

Drugs and alcohol—use and abuse

Employment rights and responsibilities; job applications

Encyclopedias and other reference tools

ESL materials

Family problems

Fantasy

Gangs

GED study course or other high school equivalency study guides

High-interest, low-level books in English

Life options (especially those beyond sports and entertainment)

Magazines and newspapers

Mystery, horror stories

Parenting issues including single parenting

Pregnancy and birth control

Psychological, emotional, and relationship issues

Romance (novels)

Sex and Sexuality

Social problems

Spanish-language literacy

Sports (find out the favorites of your patrons)

Teenage rights

Textbooks (Spanish-language)

Many of the above would also be appropriate topics for bilingual experts to speak about in settings where young people would feel free to ask questions. Diana Morales (1999) of the Houston Public Library indicated that she has arranged programs on health risks associated with tattooing and body piercing so that young people who do engage in those arts will, we hope, do so safely.

Textbooks

Spanish-language texts that supplement the school curriculum should be available to help students understand the concepts being taught. In recognition of the number of Mexican students in the United States, the Mexican government annually offers copies of official texts to schools and libraries. Requests to participate in the program should be directed to the nearest Mexican consulate or cultural center by the end of September each year. During October and November the Mexican government ships the books to six warehouses on the border.

Participating libraries and schools are required to pay only for the shipping from the border to the final U.S. destination. Copies of the texts are also available online at: http://www.sep.gob.mx.

Ephemera

As librarians, we can use our pack-rat traits to our advantage by collecting pamphlets and other ephemeral material to meet the needs of Spanish-speaking teens. Once you begin the search, aided by addresses at the ends of many of these chapters, you will find that more and more agencies are offering informational resources in English and Spanish that you can have available in the library.

■ Programming That Matters

Clashes between ethnic or cultural groups are often associated with the teenage years as teens seek to define who they are and who they want to become. Although conflicts may manifest themselves now, the roots were probably planted several years earlier when schools or communities did not validate home cultures, and diversity was not valued. If inclusion has not happened at a previous time, libraries and library staff serving these young adults should seek to be as inclusive as possible in all aspects of operation from policies to book selection to patron assistance to programming.

Computers

Libraries are often the point of access for computers, especially for lower-income families, but that may change as Web TV becomes more and more prevalent. Because young people seem to have an affinity for the new technology, we could take advantage of their interest and give them the skills to use the technology for their and our benefit. Instead of strictly library clubs, librarians should also look at technology clubs to assist students in developing their computer knowledge. More than one library relies on savvy teens to do their computer troubleshooting. This might lead into a School to Career program as well.

San Antonio Public Library's Young Adult section is a virtual library—there are no books. Jennifer Comi (1998), the Young Adult Librarian, does try to link these virtual services back to more traditional library services. The virtual Young Adult program was begun in 1997, and funded by grants from Microsoft® and the American Library Association, MCI World Com®, and an area foundation. Although Spanish-speaking teens are not specifically targeted, bilingual teens will often serve as translators for family members and friends who accompany the Spanish-speaking teens. For Hispanic Heritage Month (mid-September to mid-October), Comi emphasizes culturally relevant programming rather than Spanish or bilingual programs.

Comi finds that computer training is best done one-on-one with the youth, many of whom build their own Web pages that are then posted on the library Web site. The library orders all the Spanish-language computer and Internet books it can find through Baker & Taylor. For a summer program she has used Nickelodeon® 3D Movie Maker on CD-ROM for the students to create their own short animated movies. Everyone who participated got a certificate of participation, and a video rental store provided gift certificates for prizes. At summer's end they threw a theater party to view all the animations, with a local movie theater supplying popcorn. Because teens often get a lot of bad press, Comi likes to offer programs that give them good publicity. The Youth Wired Web Page can be viewed at: http://www.youthwired.sat.lib.tx.us.

The Branigan Library in Las Cruces, New Mexico received a grant through US West to fund its *Voces* program that emphasized Internet skills for teens. Although the kids were not much interested in the writing component of the program, the computers did bring some new teen faces into the library (Peterson 1998).

Budding Authors

The University of Houston is beginning a program, *Nuestra Palabrita,* to work through the schools to encourage and mentor teens who would like to submit literary compositions for publication. The mentors need not be famous authors, just experienced mentors. The program does hope to have a celebrity like Edward James Olmos come and speak to the young people (Morales 1999).

Another program idea would be hosting an evening coffee house where young people could read original literary compositions or play and sing original musical pieces. The one stipulation made with Rap music at the Houston Public Library is that it not contain obscenities because there are often younger children present. In addition, a talent show featuring entertainment from various cultural groups within the community could be held, perhaps as a fund-raising event (Morales 1999).

In Alamosa, Colorado, older students are building bookshelves to be placed in kindergarten through fifth grade classrooms. With help from a Service Learning Youth Ambassador Grant through the Colorado Department of Education, the students are also being encouraged to write and illustrate books to be placed on the bookshelves and to read to the younger students. Students of Spanish and native Spanish-speakers can improve their own reading skills by reading favorite stories and recording them on cassette tapes for elementary schools (Holmes 1998).

Spanish-speakers can be encouraged to submit pieces for the school newspaper, or produce radio programs to be aired locally.

Cultural Programming

A Hispanic Cultural Love-In, sponsored by the San Antonio Public Library, was held during summer of 1998 in a recreation center in a lower-income neighborhood. Local Latino artists, writers, and actors were invited to show their crafts and develop related projects with upper elementary and high school students during two days of programming (two sessions each day). Library staff tried to show how the artists might make use of the library. The program was "hugely successful for the kids and the artists."

Other programming at the San Antonio Public Library has included: fiction-writing workshops—*Palabras Jóvenes* and *Vatos Culturales; Cuentos de los Líderes de San Antone*—a panel discussion on ethnicity and leadership in which six local leaders participated; and a career workshop in which Hispanic businesspeople spoke on the importance of education and helped students fill out scholarship applications. For these programs library staff tries to use a combination of Spanish and English so both populations will understand (Payne-Button 1998).

In El Paso, Del Valle High School Library sometimes purchases and frames student artwork for display—a nice incentive for the student artists (Labodda 1998).

The Camarena Memorial Library in Calexico, California, is situated on the Mexican border with a population base that is 97 percent Hispanic. It is a given that all the staff (except one) is bilingual. The library has just begun young adult programming by encouraging youth to participate in a survey on library services; those who returned the completed survey were eligible to enter a drawing for a Karaoke machine. The newly formed Teen Council has sponsored tours and a scavenger hunt. In addition to a staff of 11, the library gets programming help through the Youth Employment Program and from students participating in the Work Study program at a nearby college.

One branch of the library is located at a junior high school. During the day it functions as a school library, and at night, with a separate staff, serves as a public library. The English- and Spanish-language materials are integrated, but do not exceed the junior high level (Tauler 1998).

Because most libraries do not have an excess of funds, they are always on the lookout for free or low-cost programs. A branch of the Houston Public Library took advantage of the fact that the nearby Art Car Museum needed a place to park some of its cars while a move took place. The library offered parking space in front of its building, and with the fanfare of balloons and radio station commentators, invited the "car artists" to come and explain their work. They even went so far as to have cheerleaders in the middle of the library to encourage library card sign-up (Morales 1999).

As a way to help all students appreciate the positive influences of Latino cultures, you could have a class of students begin collecting Spanish words that have been adopted into English. A number of words from ranching (*mustang, buckaroo, bronco, rodeo*) and mining (*placer, rastra* or *arrastra, bonanza*) come from Spanish, but there are others such as *aficionado, tango,* and *peccadillo* that are commonly used in English.

The staff of the Pikes Peak Library District in Colorado Springs, Colorado, has developed a series of skits called Funky Fairy Tales, offbeat interpretations of well-known fairy tales. Teens could develop their own variations; English, Spanish, or bilingual, with the humor geared toward the intended audience.

Miscellaneous

Hold a special reading promotion with appropriate prizes or incentives for all students during Teen Read Week in October.

Previous chapters for other relevant programming ideas: Chapter 2 discusses Job Search Clubs, conversational English/Spanish classes such as *Intercambio*, and classes for high school equivalency degrees; Chapter 3 presents some ideas for parents of young children that could also be adapted for use by teenaged parents.

■ Periodicals

These periodical titles are especially pertinent to teens, but many of the titles listed in Chapter 2 would also be appropriate. An effort has been made to provide a U.S. address for each subscription, and where that was not possible, the name of a U.S. distributor is listed.

Addresses of Distributors and Publishers

C.D.S., Subscriptions Dept.
  PO Box 37253
  Boone, IA 50037

Continental Book Company
  625 E. 70th Ave. #5
  Denver, CO 80229

  80-00 Cooper Ave. #29
  Glendale, NY 11385

EBSCO, International Headquarters
  PO Box 11943
  Birmingham, AL 35201-1943

Editorial América, S.A. (Grupo Televisa)
  6355 N.W. 36th St.
  Virginia Gardens, FL 33166 (Publisher)

Latin American Periodicals
2555 N. Coyote Dr. Suite 109
Tucson, AZ 85745

Spanish Publications Inc.
PO Box 742149
Houston, TX 77274-2149

Spanish Periodicals & Book Sales
10100 NW 25th St.
Miami, FL 33172
http://www.spanishperiodical.com

Periodical Titles

Automundo: La revista #1 del Automóvil en Español en los Estados Unidos

2960 S.W. 8th St., Second Floor
Miami, FL 33135
Distributed by EBSCO.
http://www.automundo.com

This web site would be of interest to teenage boys because it gives information on the latest car models. While the articles do focus on the makes and models of cars most popular in the United States, the latter section of the magazine deals with sports cars and racing.

Balón: Fútbol Mundial

Distributed by: EBSCO

Articles about the world of international soccer.

¡Boom! Tu Mundo Pop Latino

¡Boom!
P.O. Box 398752
Miami Beach, FL 33239
http://www.boomonline.com

A magazine all about Latino pop, rock, and alternative music.

CineManía

Cinemanía Estados Unidos
10535 Wilshire Blvd., Suite 1008
Los Angeles, CA 90024
Distributed by: Spanish Periodicals & Book Sales.

A glossy, full-color magazine published monthly covering the film world. Although heavy on Hollywood films (probably because the blockbusters tend to originate there), there are also features on European, Mexican, and other Latino films and film stars.

Cosmo Deporte Sports Magazine

Cosmo Publishing Inc.
13624 Hawthorne Blvd., Suite 210
Hawthorne, CA 90250

A full-color, glossy monthly with articles on *fútbol* (soccer), boxing, baseball, basketball, auto racing, and tennis. Men and women athletes are covered.

Deporte Ilustrado

Distributed by: EBSCO *Sports Illustrated* magazine in Spanish.

Deporte Internacional

Distributed by: Latin American Periodicals; Subscriptions: C.D.S.

A biweekly sports magazine with stories from around the world.

Discover en Español

Ideas & Capital
1101 Brickell Ave., 15th Floor
Miami, FL 33131

A monthly magazine featuring the same science articles that were in the previous month's English language issue. Some of the secondary articles are different from those in the parent magazine.

Eres: Edición USA

Editorial América, S.A. Distributed by: EBSCO; Latin American Periodicals; Continental Book Co.; Subscription: C.D.S

A biweekly magazine for teens with articles on entertainers and movie stars.

Furia Musical

Editorial América, S.A. Distributed by: Latin American Periodicals; Subscription: C.D.S.

A bimonthly publication featuring articles about musicians and musical groups, especially those with a Mexican flavor.

Geomundo

> Editorial América, S.A. Distributed by: EBSCO; Latin American Periodicals; Continental Book Co.; Subscription: C.D.S.
>
> A full-color monthly magazine with articles on science (surviving a hurricane, protective coloring in insects), ecology, worldwide destinations (Scotland, Portuguese Uruguay, Indonesian islands, etc.). Suitable for high school and up.

Latino Baseball; Latino Boxing; Latino Soccer

> King Paniagua, LLC
> 518 5th Ave. 5th Floor
> New York, NY 10036
>
> These three bilingual titles highlight Latino athletes in the respective sports. *Latino Soccer* is only published annually (July), but the other two titles appear quarterly: *Latino Baseball* in January, April, September, and December and *Latino Boxing* in February, May, September, and December.

Más Fútbol: Revista Bilingüe (Soccer America)

> Más Fútbol/Soccer America
> 1235 Tenth St.
> Berkeley, CA 94710
>
> A free publication about soccer players and their teams.

Mecánica Popular

> Editorial América, S.A. Distributed by: EBSCO; Latin American Periodicals; Subscription: C.D.S.
>
> Spanish version of the magazine *Popular Mechanics*.

México Desconocido

> Editorial México Desconocido, S.A. de C.V.
> 2544 Grandview St.
> San Diego, CA 92110
> Distributed by: EBSCO; Continental Book Co. Subscriptions:
> PO Box 371656
> San Diego, CA 92137
> http://www.mexicodesco.com
>
> A full-color monthly focusing on lesser-known Mexican customs, and off-the-beaten-track tourist destinations and adventure travel. The main audience would be people with disposable income for travel, but it could also serve to give students a greater appreciation of Mexican cultural resources and heritage.

Onda Mex

> Onda Mex
> > P.O. Box 145179
> > Coral Gables, FL 33134
> > Distributed by: Spanish Periodicals Corp.
>
> > A black-and-white publication with newsprint pages, this one covers Mexican music.

People en Español

> Distributed by:
> > Latin American Periodicals. Subscription:
> > People en Español
> > PO Box 61691
> > Tampa, FL 33661-1691
>
> > Not a translation of the English equivalent, this monthly magazines (except for the June/July and December/January issues) is written especially for Latinos in the United States. At a cost of $14.97 per year, a subscription is much more affordable for small libraries than the weekly English version.

Perspectiva Monthly: World News in Intermediate Spanish

> Educational News Service
> > PO Box 60478
> > Florence, MA 01062-0478
>
> > Geared for English-speaking students of Spanish, this 22-page digest of world news could also serve Spanish-speaking junior and senior high students who need information on current events.

15 a 20 (Quince a Veinte)

> Distributed by: Latin American Periodicals
>
> > Although titled for young women from the ages of 15 to 20, this magazine would probably appeal to younger teens. Examples of articles include makeup, the latest in shoes, bowling, sewing, underwear, and sex.

Saludos Hispanos

> Saludos Hispanos
> > 73-121 Fred Waring Dr., Suite 100
> > Palm Desert, CA 92260
> > http://www.saludos.com/saludosmagazine.html
>
> > This attractive, bimonthly, glossy magazine is the "official publication of the United Council of Spanish Speaking People."

With all the major articles in Spanish and English, the publication aims to provide young people with motivational information on careers and education. Each issue spotlights a specific area such as broadcasting or law enforcement.

Show Continental

Show Continental
PO Box 402039
Miami Beach, FL 33140

A monthly magazine with black-and-white, newsprint pages, featuring articles about popular stars from Latin America.

Sólo Soccer: El Mundo del Fútbol

Distributed by: Spanish Publications Inc.

A monthly magazine about the best teams and players in the world of soccer (*fútbol* in Spanish).

Somos Uno

Distributed by: Latin American Periodicals

A bimonthly Mexican magazine about movies and the people who star in them. Examples of articles include: history of the bolero, Evita, La Amistad, Alec Baldwin and Kim Basinger, and Sophia Loren and Carlo Ponti.

■ Works Cited

Alire, Camila and Orlando Archibeque. *Serving Latino Communities: A How-To-Do-It Manual for Librarians*. New York: Neal-Schuman, 1998.

Anstrom, Kris. *Preparing Secondary Education Teachers to Work with English Language Learners: Science*. Washington, D.C.: George Washington University, 1998.

Comi, Jennifer. Telephone interview with author, 14 Oct. 1998.

Dame, Melvina Azar. *The Role of the School Library in Serving LEP/ESL Students*. 1994. ERIC. (ED 381033).

Headden, Susan. "The Hispanic Dropout Mystery: A Staggering 30 Percent Leave School, Far More Than Blacks or Whites. Why?" *U.S. News & World Report* (20 Oct.1998): 64+.

Holmes, Nora. Personal conversation with author, Colorado Springs, Colo., 29 Oct. 1998.

Krashen, Stephen. Why Consider the Library and Books? In *Literacy, Access, and Libraries Among the Language Minority Population,* edited by Rebecca Constantino. Lanham, Md.: Scarecrow Press, 1998.

Labodda, Marsha J. Personal communication, 17 June 1998.

Latin American Research and Service Agency. *LARASA/Report: A Publication About Latinos in Colorado* (June 1998).

McQuillan, Jeff and Victoria Rodrigo. Literature-Based Programs for First Language Development: Giving Native Bilinguals Access to Books. In *Literacy, Access, and Libraries Among the Language Minority Population,* edited by Rebecca Constantino. Lanham, Md.: Scarecrow Press, 1998.

Mendosa, Rick. "What's Up With Teenagers?" *Hispanic Business* (July-Aug. 1998): 58–62.

Minicucci, Catherine and Laurie Olsen. *Programs for Secondary Limited English Proficient Students: A California Study.* Washington, D.C.: National Clearinghouse for Bilingual Education, 1992.

Mora, Pat. Personal interview with author, Steamboat Springs, Colo., 12 Sept. 1998.

Morales, Diana. Telephone conversation with author, 26 March 1999.

Navarrette, Yolanda Gómez. "Family Involvement in a Bilingual School," *The Journal of Educational Issues of Language Minority Students* (Summer 1996). [On-line] Available: http://www.ncbe.gwu.edu/miscpubs/jeilms/vol16/jeilms1606.htm (Accessed Dec. 14, 1998).

Payne-Button, Linda. Telephone interview with author, 13 Oct. 1998.

Peterson, Verla. Personal conservation with author, Taos, N.M., 31 Oct. 1998

Rodriguez, Judith. "Books for Young Adults: Libros Para Adolescentes," *REFORMA Newsletter* (Summer 1995): 7.

Sanchez, Saadia et al. *Public Library Services for Latino Young Adults.* Berkeley: University of California School of Library and Information Studies, 1989.

Tauler, Sandra. Telephone interview with author, 22 Oct. 1998.

Chapter 6

Communicating with Patrons

■ Accessing the Resources

Helping new or potential Spanish-speaking patrons feel comfortable in the library means speaking a language they understand and giving them the tools to figure out some things for themselves. The challenge can be twofold. First, they need to understand in their first language how a library functions and where different kinds of information/services are located: Where is the bathroom? Where are the Spanish-language magazines? Does anyone here speak Spanish? However if they are not familiar with a library at all, they may not understand the meaning of unique library terms such as *call number* or *on-line catalog*, even if the proper Spanish words are used.

To give a consistent good impression, all signage, forms, and instructions should be in Spanish. In preparing to write this book, I took a look around my library and realized the signage was not as bilingual as it could be. It might help to have a friend peruse your building and suggest possible signage improvements from an independent perspective.

Some people feel that if a library program is aimed mainly at monolingual Spanish-speakers, publicity and/or signs should only be in Spanish to avoid giving the impression that they are being served as an afterthought. On the other hand, bilingual publicity could target two populations at once. Appendix B of this book contains examples of information pieces that you are free to adapt. Be extremely careful of computer programs that do translations, as they can produce disastrous results that are next to incomprehensible or give very wrong impressions.

■ Spanish Language

Spanish is a very phonetic language with fewer silent letters or exceptions to the rules than English. The principal in a bilingual elementary school in Colorado remarked that students would much rather take spelling tests in Spanish for that very reason. It is a sign of respect for Spanish-speakers and their culture to use Spanish that is grammatically correct with proper spelling, especially in written communications. Otherwise, you may risk giving the impression that you were not concerned enough to find out how to write the words properly.

Accent Marks

Unlike French, where accent marks indicate differences in the pronunciation of vowels, in Spanish they indicate which syllable to stress when a word does not follow one of the standard rules, which are:

1. Unless a word ends in a vowel, "s", or "n", the stress falls on the last syllable. Examples include, with the stressed syllable in bold: au-**tor** to-**mar** pe-**dir** verti-**cal**

2. For words ending in a vowel, "s", or "n", the stress falls on the next to the last syllable. Examples: biblio-**te**-ca **li**-bro **at**-las **jo**-ven

3. Words that have stressed syllables not following rules one or two will need an accent mark. Examples: ca-**tá**-logo **nú**-mero ficc-**ión**

More and more frequently I observe Spanish words in print that have incorrectly placed accent marks. To further emphasize, a stressed syllable does NOT need an accent mark if it follows the first two rules. Also, letters of the alphabet printed in capital letters may not have accent marks noted above them.

Many library computer programs do not support the use of diacritics; however, if possible, use them. Some words do change meanings depending on which syllable is stressed. For example:

es-ta means "this" but *es-tá* means "he, she or it is";

li-bro means "book" but *li-bró* means "he, she or it saved (freed)" something;

la pa-pa means "potato"; *el pa-pa* means "the pope"; but *el pa-pá* means "father".

Articles

Just as in English, articles at the beginnings of titles are ignored when alphabetizing: The = *el, la, los, las* (masculine singular, feminine singular, masculine plural, feminine plural); A, an = *un, una* (masculine singular, feminine singular). To be grammatically correct, the online catalog should disregard initial articles and patrons should be instructed to begin a title search with the next significant word.

Names

Spanish or Latino names can also be confusing. Many people use two last names, as does author Gabriel García Márquez. The first last name, García, is his paternal last name, and the name under which all his works should be alphabetized. The second, Márquez, is his maternal last name (equivalent to his mother's maiden name and the name passed down through her father's family). If one had to choose one last name by which to refer to him, it would be Señor García, **not** Señor Márquez. However, Jorge Luis Borges uses a first, middle, and last name, so his works would be filed under B. Women may keep their maiden names as Rigoberta Menchú Tum, Nobel Peace Prize winner from Guatemala (who would be alphabetized under "M" and not "T") , or use a combination of their own and their husband's names as Violeta Barrios de Chamorro (literally "de Chamorro" means wife of Chamorro), former president of Nicaragua.

For a further explanation of Spanish names, see the 17th chapter of *The Chicago Manual of Style*, 14th edition (1993). The introduction to *Bilindex* (see later in this chapter) also gives a good explanation of Spanish names and how they should be alphabetized.

■ OPACs

Online Public Access Catalogs (OPACs) make it easier for researchers who want to search many databases in a timely fashion, or who want to search from home or office, but these catalogs may make access more difficult for patrons with limited English ability and little or no knowledge of computers. Several libraries have attempted to make their online services friendly to speakers of other languages but it is still important to make your Spanish-language collection readily visible and easy to browse. Viewing some of the online catalogs noted later can give library staff an idea of how other libraries have approached Spanish-language access from their OPACs. Some of the sites also allow access to Machine Readable Cataloging (MARC) records for their holdings.

As an example, the Los Angeles Public Library's CARLweb interface has a Spanish-language option (http://catalog.lapl.org:80/). The directions on the main screen are in Spanish, as are the labeled elements of screens with bibliographic data. However, the summaries (*Resúmenes*) included with children's titles are in English, as are the subject headings.

In contrast, the San Antonio Public Library that also uses a version of CARLweb (http://saplweb.sat.lib.tx.us), has no Spanish directions on its initial screen, and the screen element labels are in English. Once a patron chooses the Public Catalog option, that patron will find that summaries and subject headings are in English and Spanish. In addition, CARL Corporation offers a Spanish version of its Kid's Catalog that can be used with several stand-alone library automation systems.

The Fort Collins (Colo.) Public Library (http://dalva.fcgov.com) is an Innovative Interfaces, Inc. (III) system where patrons can choose "Spanish Collection" from the main menu. Subject headings are in English and Spanish, and if pertinent, the word "*Español*" appears in the location field.

The Kansas City (Mo.) Public Library's (KCPL) online catalog, a DRA (Data Research Associates, Inc.) system, lists *Español* as one of the choices of a "branch" to search. Once that selection has been made, all the screen helps are in Spanish. Subject headings for Spanish-language titles are given in English and Spanish. The URL for the KCPL Online Catalog is: http://web2.kclibrary.org.

The Queens Borough Public Library in Jamaica, New York (http://web.queens.lib.ny.us8004) which also uses a DRA system, has good initial screens in Spanish including "Helps" explaining how to conduct searches. Subject headings are in English and Spanish, but most title level information is in English.

The Web page for the Newark (N.J.) Public Library, an epixtech system, (http://www.npl.org/Pages/Spanish/index.html) offers a Spanish version of information about its collection, services, and cultural programming. Catalog helps are all in English, but subject headings are also given in Spanish.

SIRS Mandarin M3 Web Gateway offers catalog interfaces in a choice of English, Spanish, or French. The system can be viewed at: http://webmandarin.sirs.com/M3.

Follett Software advertises Language Pack, an "add-on module to Catalog Plus for MS-DOS" that allows patrons to search the library catalog in English, French, or Spanish. Access information at: http://www.fsc.follett.com.

First Search, a database from Online Computer Library Center, Inc. (OCLC), is an example of a database that allows patrons to switch between interfaces in English, French, and Spanish. This would be a resource for checking Spanish-language subject headings used for bilingual or Spanish books (see more later).

Although the interface with the Alameda County (Calif.) Library is in English, their online catalog does show the variety of languages in which they can collect materials. The catalog, an Innovative Interfaces, Inc. system, can be accessed at: http://aclibrary.org.

Inevitably, however, no matter how well a library does with initial screens, at some point most patrons arrive at screens with English only. If there is a clientele with very limited English, it might help to display printed signs with the equivalent English/Spanish computer terms (see Appendix B).

Addresses

CARL Corporation
   3801 E. Florida, Suite 300
   Denver, CO 80210
   1-888-439-CARL
   http://www.carl.org

DRA (Data Research Associates)
   1276 N. Warson Rd.
   St. Louis, MO 63132
   1-800-325-0888
   http://www.dra.com

epixtech (formerly Dynix)
   400 West 5050 North
   Provo, UT 84604
   1-800-288-8020
   http://www.epixtech.com

Follett Software Company
   1391 Corporate Dr.
   McHenry, IL 60050-7041
   1-800-323-3397
   http://www.fsc.follett.com

Innovative Interfaces, Inc.
   5850 Shellmound Way
   Emeryville, CA 94608
   510-655-6200
   http://www.iii.com

OCLC, Inc.
   6565 Frantz Rd.
   Dublin, OH 43017
   1-800-848-5878
   http://www.oclc.org

SIRS Mandarin, Inc.
   P.O. Box 272348
   Boca Raton, FL 33427-2728
   1-800-232-7477
   http://www.sirs.com

■ Cataloging

For a librarian not familiar with Spanish, the wording on a title page or its verso can be confusing, especially if you must do your own original cataloging. The parts of a sample title page are explained in Appendix B, and will help in sorting things out.

Subject Headings

Because the online or card catalog is the main location tool for patrons, libraries should consider adding Spanish subject headings for all Spanish-language materials. The main subject heading tool, based on Library of Congress subject headings, is *Bilindex* (1984) and its supplements in which one can look up the appropriate English subject heading and find the Spanish equivalent, or vice versa. *Bilindex* can be ordered from Floricanto Press. Not cheap, especially for small libraries, a group of neighboring libraries might consider buying and sharing one copy.

To supplement *Bilindex*, and fill in gaps, the Oakland and San Francisco Public Libraries have a Web site (http://clnet.ucr.edu/library/bplg/sujetos.htm) listing Spanish-language subject headings they have created.

One or more of the following subjects (in addition to more specific ones) might be appropriate if a library wanted to have Spanish-language materials readily findable under a few headings:

Spanish-language materials

Bilingual books—English-Spanish

Bilingual text

Libros bilingües—Inglés-Español

For nonfiction books, the words (*in Spanish*) could be added to English-language subject tracings and the word *Bilingüe* or *Bilingual* could be added to the subject tracings to indicate that two languages are represented.

Location Tools

Probably the easiest way for patrons with limited English proficiency to find needed material is to browse the shelves. A prominently placed poster of the Dewey Decimal Classification system in Spanish or Spanish and English would help. Libraries use the following techniques, or combinations, to identify Spanish-language books:

For libraries using MARC format or other online databases, a designation can be placed in the format and/or location fields to indicate Spanish language or bilingual. Some libraries place an "S" or "SPA" at the beginning of the call number, while others put SPA, SPANISH, or ESPAÑOL after it.

Spine Labels

1. Florescent, brightly colored stickers that say: ESPAÑOL, SPANISH, ESPAÑOL/SPANISH, LIBROS EN ESPAÑOL, BILINGUAL/ BILINGÜE, ESL.

2. Colored adhesive strip on spine.

3. Genre labels could be used in addition to either of the first two labels.

Location

1. All Spanish-language materials shelved together in one section, preferably easily accessible to the entrance. The section could be marked: ESPAÑOL, LIBROS (MATERIA) EN ESPAÑOL, MATERIALES PARA LA GENTE DE HABLA ESPAÑOLA, SPANISH LANGUAGE, BILINGUAL/BILINGÜE, ESL. (My personal preference would be one of the first three designations. The term "Bilingual" could refer to any number of language combinations, not just English and Spanish; ESL implies that the patron is trying to learn English as a Second Language, which may not necessarily be the case.) One drawback to this option is that if a group of Spanish-speakers come to the library at the same time, they would all be trying to simultaneously access the same small section of books whereas English speakers can spread out throughout the rest of the library. Bilingual materials might be shelved along with other materials for the targeted population.

2. The elementary school library in Ft. Lupton, Colorado, has low sectional bookshelves (three shelves per unit), and the Spanish books are placed adjacent to the English-language books of the same call number range. That way, all students seeking information on elephants would go to the same section of the library, but they would not be competing for space with others looking for folk tales.

3. Completely intersperse the Spanish-language materials with the regular collection, using spine labels as the major differentiation. This method does not single out patrons seeking materials in a specific language and may help those who are fluent in more than one language. It may be best for libraries with substantial collections of Spanish-language materials or whose patrons are primarily bilingual.

■ Addendum

The following article is reprinted with permission from the author. It was originally published in the Fall 1998 issue of *La Herencia del Norte* (Gran Via, Inc., P.O. Box 22576, Santa Fe, NM 87502; 505-474-2800; http://www.herencia.com)

Emphasis on the Accent by A. Samuel Adelo

We learn our first language when we are babies by imitating the people around us. Under normal conditions, after a period of babbling, babies learn to articulate words that they need for their relations with others. It is not necessary for a baby to learn many words to acquire the phonetic articulation of her/his own native language. From that time on, learning the language will last a lifetime, and it will only be a matter of adding elements, repeating and forming associations.

Early on, the position of the stressed syllable becomes fixed in the mind of the child who is learning a first language. This is so even as the child learns words with emphasis on different syllables. In English, for example, in the word *father* the syllable "fa" is emphasized. In the word *alone*, it's the syllable "lone" that gets the emphasis. In English there are no fixed rules for the stressed syllable in spoken words.

In many languages the position of the stressed syllable is fixed. In spoken Spanish, the emphasis of the syllable varies in different words. Consequently, the written accent is an integral part of correct Spanish spelling. Likewise the use of *ü* and the *ñ*.

Many people nowadays have a propensity to leave out the written accent, the diaeresis, and to substitute *n* for *ñ* in Spanish words.

To pronounce the word correctly, the written accent indicates to the reader the syllable that should be stressed when the word does not follow the rules. The *ñ* is simply the 17th letter of the Spanish alphabet. The diaeresis is required when the *u* should be pronounced and should not remain silent.

Respect for Hispanic people and their language demands that the accent, the *ñ* and the *ü* be written in certain Spanish words. In proper names, it is not only respect for the language but also for the person that demands that the accent and the *ñ* be used.

In spoken Spanish, there are three simple rules that tell you which syllable to emphasize. Those rules are:

Rule 1:   If a word ends in *a, o, u, e, i, n,* or *s,* the emphasis is placed on the next-to-the-last syllable. Examples of such words are: som-**bre**-ro, co-**mi**-da, **sie**-te, **qui**-nce, **lu**-nes, se-**ño**-ra.

Rule 2:   If a word ends in a consonant other than *n* or *s*, the emphasis is on the last syllable. Examples of such words are se-**ñor**, ho-**tel**, fa-**vor**, I-sa-**bel**, us-**ted**, cam-**biar**.

Rule 3:   If the emphasis does not follow Rules 1 or 2, an accent mark indicates what syllable will be emphasized when that word in spoken. Examples of such words are **sá**-bado, **miér**-coles, **Gó**-mez, Jo-**sé**, ja-**bón**, au-to-**mó**-vil.

Examples of Spanish proper names that have an accent are Jo-**sé**, Ra-**món**, Mar-**tín**, Ma-**ría**, **Bár**-ba-ra, and Ad-**án**. Examples of Spanish surnames that have an accent are **Sán**-chez, Mar-**tín**-ez, A-ra-**gón**, **Ló**-pez, Val-**dés**, Gar-**cía**, **Juá**-rez.

Improper pronunciation is particularly noticeable in the way many broadcasters pronounce the Spanish surnames of certain major league baseball players.

The evolution of computer use in the global village we live in makes it easy to write the accent. The *ñ*, and for that matter multinational characters and diacritics, are now available in most computer systems. The proper use of such diacritics clearly is a reflection of a person's cultural level and sensitivity for other peoples' language systems. On the other hand, refusal to use the accepted diacritics of other languages, particularly in given names and surnames, reflects a narrow bias and mistaken attitude.

■ Works Cited

Adelo, A. Samuèl. "Emphasis on the Accent," *La Herencia del Norte* (Fall 1998): 54.

Bilindex: A Bilingual Spanish-English Subject Heading List. Oakland, Calif.: California Spanish Language Data Base, 1984.

The Chicago Manual of Style. 14th edition. Chicago: University of Chicago Press, 1993.

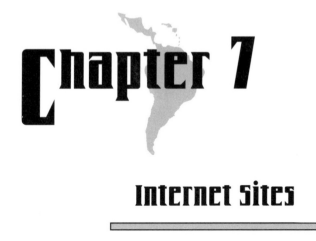

Chapter 7

Internet Sites

Although the World Wide Web should not substitute for having Spanish-language materials readily available in the library, it can provide a source for supplemental materials and patrons may be able to access information directly from their home countries. Because many of these sites link to English and Spanish resources, they could also serve students of any background who are participating in cultural studies.

■ Internet Tutorials

Aprenda la Red (Learn the Web): http://www.learnthenet.com/spanish/index.html

An Internet tutorial available in English, French, German, Italian, and Spanish.

La Red Desenredada: Una Guía Introductoria al Internet (The Web Unraveled: An Introductory Guide to the Internet): http://www.civila.com/desenredada/ index.htm

A guide to the Web for the nontechnical person.

Tejedores del Web - Aprendiendo a diseñar páginas Web (Spinners of the Web - Learning to Design Web Pages): http://www.TejedoresDelWeb.com

An HTML manual for designing Web pages. Tutorial de Internet: http://lg.msn.com/intl/es/tutorial

Microsoft's® Internet tutorial in Spanish.

Writing HTML: Un Tutorial Para Crear Páginas WWW: http://www. mcli.dist.maricopa.edu/tut_es

Another tutorial in Spanish, this one is especially aimed at teachers who wish to create Web tools using HTML programming language.

■ E-Mail

If your library has enough computers with Internet connections to allow patrons to use e-mail, this service can be one that draws people to the facility, especially if they do not have Internet access at home or their place of employment. The following is a list of free e-mail services (*E-mails gratis*):

Yupi Internet: http://www.yupi.com

Free e-mail aimed at the Spanish-speaking market. Yupi also provides an area for translating Internet URLs from one language to another.

Ciudad Futura: http://www.ciudadfutura.net

Lists free e-mail services in English (21 addresses) and Spanish (six addresses).

Léttera: http://www.lettera.net

A free e-mail service from Spain promoting itself for the lack of advertising sent with posted messages.

MixMail: http://www6.mixmail.com

Another free e-mail source.

Hotmail: http://www.hotmail.com

Although instructions are not given in Spanish, Hotmail does seem to be a popular source of free e-mail for many people, English-speakers or not.

■ Search Engines

Altavista®: http://www.altavista.com

Altavista® allows for Web pages to be translated into several different languages, including Spanish. The results are not always grammatically correct, however.

Babelfish: http://babelfish.altavista.digital.com

Translation software that allows patrons to enter plain text or a URL and receive a translation.

CiberCentro: http://www.cibercentro.com

Available in English and Spanish, this site provides links to directories and search engines in Spanish-speaking countries. Links are arranged by country.

Spain: http://www.ozu.es

A Spanish search engine with links categorized under such headings as Science and Technology, Culture, Sports, Ecology, and Education.

Spanish Language Search Engines: http://www.escapeartist.com/search4/buscalo.html

A listing of Latin-American and Spanish-language Search Engines that is mostly in Spanish.

Terra: http://www.terra.es

A diverse site from Spain with links to a wide variety of subjects including News, Science, Film, Education, and Music. One caution is that a few levels down in the Art section are artworks labeled as pornographic. While many adults would not have a problem with them, they are probably not suitable for minors.

Yahoo!®: http://espanol.yahoo.com

Besides having links categorized by subject, Yahoo! ® in Spanish links to sites in Argentina, Chile, Colombia, Spain, Mexico, Peru, and Venezuela as well as countries in Europe, Asia, and Australia/New Zealand.

■ Pathfinders: Older Students & Adults

Aztlánnet: http://www.aztlannet.com

> A source of Latino, Chicano, and Native American art and literary work. Although all text is in English, the artwork could be appreciated by any interested person.

Bibliotecas Para La Gente: http://clnet.ucr.edu/library/bplg

> Bibliotecas Para La Gente is a chapter of REFORMA serving the people of northern California. The site has links to Booktalk, storytime, and Latino program ideas, and Search Engines in English and Spanish. It is also the home of Oakland Public Library/San Francisco Public Library Spanish Subject Headings: http://clnet.ucr.edu/library/.htm

CLNet (Chicano/Latino Net) Home Page: http://latino.sscnet.ucla.edu

> Geared more toward Latinos for whom English is their first language, this site has links to such Web resources as Publishers and Bookstores, Virtual Libraries and Museums, Listservs, and Research Collections as well as Art, Music, Dance, and Theater and Film.

Hispanic Online's Latino Links: http://www.hisp.com/links.html

> Many of the links on this commercial site sponsored by Hispanic Publishing Corp. are in English, but there are also links to Web sites in Latin America. Subject areas covered include Politics, Arts, Lifestyles, Business, and Career and Education.

Hispanic Pages in the USA: http://coloquio.com

> Although many of the links are in English, there are also links to Latin American countries and Spain, a list of famous Hispanics, and information on bullfighting.

Hot Links: http://www.eldish.net/hp/flashram/Hotlinks.htm

> Geared mainly toward young people, these links are to Web browsers, popular musical groups, television channels, and sports sites.

Internet Resources for Latin America, Spain, and Portugal: http://dizzy. library.arizona.edu/users/ppromis/patricia.htm

> Included in the links from this URL are: Mega Sites, Chicano/Hispanio Border Studies, Civilizations of Latin America, Economic Development, Government and Political Science, Films and Cinema, and the Spanish language. Information in Spanish, English, and Portuguese is included.

Latin American Network Information Center (LANIC): http://lanic. utexas.edu

> Links categorized under: countries, subjects, LANIC projects, regional resources, and global resources.

Los Angeles Public Library: http://www.lapl.org/spanish/lared.html

> A large selection of Web links for older students and adults in such areas as Art, Technology, Film, Popular Culture, Food, Employment, Immigration, Music, Health, and more.

REFORMA National Web Site: http://www.reforma.org/refochpt.htm

> For general information about REFORMA: The National Association to Promote Library Services to the Spanish Speaking, as well as a listing of local chapters.

REFORMA-Colorado: http://carbon.cudenver.edu/public/library/reforma

> Provides links especially useful for Latinos in Colorado.

REFORMA Heartland Chapter: http://www.skyways.org/orgs/reforma/ hearthom.html

> Composed of library staff from Kansas and the Kansas City area of Missouri, the Heartland Chapter's Web site links to Subject Indexes and Directories, ESL material, and information for families and librarians.

REFORMA Nevada Chapter: www.clan.lib.nv.us/docs/reforma/ links.htm

> Besides information about the local chapter, the Nevada Web page includes a listing of Spanish newspapers on the Web and the Library Bill of Rights in Spanish.

REFORMA Northeast Chapter: http://reforma-northeast.org

> Lists libraries in the Northeast with Home Pages in Spanish. Some of those have links to other sites pertinent to the Latino community.

Red de Recursos Hispanos (Hispanic Resources Web): http://www.lib. panam.edu/~web3/redhisp.html

> Includes listings for Academic Sites, The Arts, Bilingual Resources, Business Resources, Correo Electrónico, Cyberspace Info, Hispanic Organizations, Hispanic War heroes, Indexes/Pathfinders/Search Engines/Directories, Language/Grammar/Dictionaries, Latin America, Libraries, Mexico, Online Periodicals, Spain, Spanish Language Classes, and Traditions and Customs.

Saint Paul Public Library: Sitios en Español: http://www.lib.mn.us/pages/ pubpg/sitiosen.htm

> Spanish Web links provided to the public include Search Engines from Mexico, Argentina, Chile, and Venezuela, e-mail, news, general sites, computer-related sites, and ESL/Citizenship resources.

Spanish Language and Culture: http://polyglot.lss.wisc.edu/lss/lang/ span/spanlink.html

> Connections to a variety of sites in Latin America and Spain dealing with such subjects as cuisine, arts and entertainment, museums, music, city/country tours, and news sources.

Vanderbilt University: Resources for Spanish Language and Literature: http://www.library.vanderbilt.edu/central/span.html#spanlat

> Links to libraries in Spain and Latin America and other sites in those countries, Spanish-language newspapers and magazines, and general language resources.

Web Information about Latinos: http://www.atm-info.com/pathfind.htm

> Connects to English- and Spanish-language sites in the subject areas of Theater, Population, Music/Dance, Politics/Law, Health, Business, Folklore, and more.

■ Other Sites of Interest

Adults and Older Students

Amigos (Friends): http://www.kn.pacbell.com/wired/amigos/spanish.htm

> Sponsored by San Diego State University and Pacific Bell Education, and available in English and Spanish, Amigos is a Web site geared toward the needs of upper elementary and older students. The page offers information on such topics as drugs and addiction, mental health, and ethnic diversity.

Cultures of the Andes: http://www.andes.org

> Information about Peru, Bolivia, Argentina, Ecuador, Colombia, and Chile in Quechua with translations into English and Spanish.

Day of the Dead: http://daphne.palomar.edu/muertos

> Links to some English and some Spanish sites for the Day of the Dead celebration held annually at the beginning of November.

Diego Rivera: Virtual Museum: http://www.diegorivera.com

> This site provides information on Mexican muralist Diego Rivera.

Discovery Channel®: http://www.salud.discoveryespanol.com/saludhome2.html

> Lists the broadcast schedule of the Discovery Channel in Spanish, with descriptions of the programs.

EBSCO: http://www.epnet.com

> Ebsco has full-text databases with Spanish interfaces on CD-ROM that are suitable for school libraries.

Edusat: http://edusat.ilce.edu.mx

> Edusat broadcasts a number of educational and cultural programs via satellite from Mexico. These are already available in southern parts of the United States, and projections are that they will soon be available in all parts of this country. Contact the nearest Mexican embassy or Cultural Center to find out when this might be available in your area, and to secure the satellite coordinates.

Food and Drug Administration (FDA) Center for Food Safely and Applied Nutrition: http://vm.cfsan.fda.gov/~mow/sinterna.html

Information from the FDA, in Spanish, on such topics as cosmetics, food additives, labeling, pesticides, and seafood.

Grupo Anaya: http://www.anaya.es/diccionario/indice.htm

The publishing group from Spain provides two online dictionaries: *Diccionario Anaya de la Lengua*, geared toward students, and *Diccionario General de la Lengua Vox* for more advanced learners or readers of Spanish. Buttons allow for translations from English to Spanish and vice versa. There is also a guide to Spanish film, searchable by title, director, and actors.

Healthfinder®: http://www.healthfinder.gov/justforyou/espanol/default.htm

Useful information to help the consumer better understand and treat diabetes and conditions leading to infant mortality.

Hispano Music & Culture of the Northern Rio Grande: The Juan B. Rael Collection: http://memory.loc.gov/ammem/rghtml/rghome.html

A Library of Congress collection of essays documenting religious and secular music of the Northern Rio Grande region. Some of the text is in English, some in Spanish.

Informe: (The Gale Group): http://galegroup.com

Available through GaleNet by subscription, *Informe* is a periodical index with some full-text access to Spanish-language periodical articles.

Language Links: http://polyglot.lss.wisc.edu/lss/lang/langlink.html

The University of Wisconsin-Madison offers ideas for teachers and learners of several languages for using materials found on this and other Web sites.

LatinoLink: http://www.latino.com

An abstracting service of Latino-related news with sections in English and Spanish.

Latino Online News Network: http://www.latnn.com

News from and about Latin America; many of the stories are in English, as are helps on the page.

Lesson Plans: http://ladb.unm.edu/retanet/plans

> Included are 65 lesson plans for secondary educators dealing with aspects of life in Latin America and the Caribbean.

Mental Health: www.mentalhealth.org/espanol

> The U.S. Department of Health and Human Services provides resources for Spanish-speakers including two publications: *Caring for Every Child's Mental Health: Communities Together* and *How are You?* which are available from the Web page, or by calling a toll-free telephone number.

Mexico Web: http://mexico.web.com.mx

> Links to a number of sites in Mexico including such aspects as Art and culture, Science and technology, Computers, Education, Business, Entertainment, Government, and Newspapers and television.

Mundo Latino: http://www.mundolatino.org/index.htm

> Provides links to sites of interest to older students and adults dealing with all the Hispanic Countries, Music, Literature, Art, Magazines, Newspapers and Radio Stations, and Political Analysis.

Musée: Directory of World-Wide Museums: http://www.musee-online. org

> Links to home pages of museums from around the world including some in Spain and Latin America.

National Center for Missing and Exploited Children: http://www. missingkids.com

> Oriented toward parents and other adult caregivers, this site offers suggestions, including publications that can be downloaded, on youth protection.

National Clearinghouse for Alcohol and Drug Information: http://www. health.org/hisp99/commenu.htm

> User-friendly and written in an easy-to-understand style, the Hispanic/Latino Initiative Materials would be valuable for students and adults.

National Coalition for Cancer Survivorship: http://www.cansearch.org/spanish/index.html

> The NCCS offers its Web site in English and Spanish. Included in the selections are Programs for Survivors and Public Health Topics.

National Crime Prevention Council: http://www.ncpc.org

> Gives tips for being secure in various settings, in English and Spanish. Safety booklets and posters can also be purchased.

National Heart, Lung, and Blood Institute: http://www.nhlbi.nih.gov/health/public/heart/index.htm

> Latino Resources is one of the options at the top of this Web page. Among resources available online are English/Spanish booklets on heart health.

National Institute of Mental Health: http://www.nimh.nih.gov

> Information in Spanish can be found by doing a search under the word *Español* or by clicking on Outline, and then going to the heading: Public Information.

National Latino Communication Center: http:/www.nlcc.com/progdev2.htm

> The aim of the NLCC is to assist in the production and distribution of films and television programs portraying Latinos in a realistic light.

NOAH: New York Online Access to Health Home Page: http://www.noah.cuny.edu

> Health-related resources in English and Spanish.

El Nuevo Herald (Miami): http://www.elherald.com

> Spanish-language newspaper with breaking stories online.

OCLC's First Search: http://www.oclc.org/oclc/menu/fs.htm

> A subscription database, it does have an option for searching in Spanish.

OCLC Links to Latin America: http://www.oclc.org/america_latina/ new_libs.htm

    For students who might want to get a glimpse of higher education in other parts of the world, OCLC provides links to selected universities in Latin America and the Caribbean.

Organization of American States (OAS)/Organización de los Estados Americanos: http://www.oas.org/defaultS.asp

    Home page of the OAS with text available in English or Spanish.

Planned Parenthood: http://www.plannedparenthood.org/Library/ PPFA-LIBRARY/SpanishSexEd.HTM

    A list of Spanish-language resources on sexuality and other health issues.

Political Database of the Americas: Georgetown University/Organization of American States: http://www.georgetown.edu/pdba

    Connections to official documents of countries in the Americas.

Puerto Rico's home page: http://fortaleza.govpr.org

    Offers information on Puerto Rico's government, tourism, weather, and official statistics.

La Raza: Bilingual Hispanic online newspaper in Chicago: http:// www.laraza.com

    National and international news stories are covered.

Templo Mayor Museum (Mexico City): http://archaeology.la.asu.edu/tm

    The rooms of this virtual museum are dedicated to various aspects of life of the Mexican people of ancient Mexico with hypertext links to further explanations of specific concepts and terms, and photos. In English and Spanish.

Teotihuacán (Mexico): http://archaeology.la.asu.edu/teo

    This site, which Arizona State University has posted with English text, details the archaeological ruins of the Pyramids of the Sun and the Moon at Teotihuacán.

25 Most Powerful Hispanics in Hollywood: http://www.hisp.com/apr96/25most.html

In English, and sponsored by *Hispanic* and *Moderna* magazines, this site gives info on some of the Hispanic Hollywood stars about whom young people want to know.

Virtual Libraries Museum Pages: http://nic.icom.org/vlmp

The pages for museums in Spanish-speaking countries are in Spanish, so students could check them to find out information about the cultural and historical resources of those countries.

Webmuseum of Latinamerica: http://museos.web.com.mx

Links to Latin American museum Web sites, including several in Portuguese.

For Children

Actividades Para Niños: http://www.fceusa.com/ninos/ninos.htm

Although some of the activities include writing, drawing, and reading contests, there is a trivia game online as well as links to other sites.

Espacio Infantil de Venezuela (Venezuelan Children's Space): http://www.ven.net/espacio

Presents a collection of four children's stories by Dr. Roberto Sánchez.

Los Angeles Public Library: http://www.lapl.org/kidsweb/spanish/index-e.html

Children's Page of the Los Angeles Public Library: Web sites especially suited for children selected by library staff. Includes a mixture of pages in English and Spanish, but those only in English are marked with a special symbol.

Lugares en Español Para Niños (Sites in Spanish for Children): http://www.ala.org/parentspage/greatsites/arts2.html#g

The Children and Technology Committee of the Association of Library Service for Children, a division of the American Library Association, collected the resources on this site, aimed at preschoolers through 14 year olds.

National Clearinghouse for Alcohol and Drug Information: http://w3.
arrakis.es/iea/kids/kids.htm

> A Spanish version of the "Just Say No" campaign to create
> awareness of the hazards of drug and alcohol abuse, with links to
> related sites in English and Spanish.

National Museum of American Art: http://nmaa-ryder.si.edu/webzine/
index.html

> Although this site is in English, it does have a collection of
> art by Latino artists that could be appreciated by many.

Los Niños e Internet 99 (Children and Internet 99): http://www.ua-
cam.mx/peques99/entrada.htm

> Some fun activities for children in the areas of video games,
> movies, foods, sports, animals, and science.

Recursos Educativos para Profesores (Educational Resources for
Teachers): http://ciervo.conce.plaza.cl

> When reviewed, this Chilean site listed teacher Internet re-
> sources on a topic of interest to students of all ages—in this case
> "Our Rivers." The majority of links are to Spanish-language
> sites, but those in English were so marked.

Red Escolar (School Net): http://www.redesc.ilce.edu.mx

> *Red Escolar* is an Internet-based supplement to the Mexican
> educational system. Under the Library (*Biblioteca*) link, students
> can find such resources as the results of Mexican students' re-
> search projects, a list of Mexican newspapers on the Internet,
> texts of stories and tales, and photos of school children participat-
> ing in the project in Mexico.

El Rinconcito (The Little Corner): http://www.mundolatino.org/rin-
concito/index.htm

> One area of the Mundo Latino Web pages has activities for
> children including "magical stories."

Appendix A
Helps for Librarians

■ Selection Tools

Bookbird: World of Children's Books. Journal of the IBBY, International Board on Books for Young People

Bookbird
> P. O. Box 807
> Highland Park, IL 60035-0807

> A quarterly publication, issues of *Bookbird* feature a column: "International Children's Books of Note" which often includes titles from specific Spanish-speaking countries.

Booklist

Booklist
> 434 W. Downer
> Aurora, IL 60506
> http://ala.ala.org/booklist

> In addition to the occasional review of a bilingual book in the regular sections of the magazine, *Booklist* features about five columns per year on Spanish-language books for children and adults. Isabel Schon writes the columns on children's books.

Bulletin of the Center for Children's Books

> Graduate School of Library and Information Science of University of Illinois at Urbana-Champaign
> 1325 S. Oak
> Champaign, IL 61820

> Published monthly except August this magazine does review some bilingual children's books.

Center for the Study of Books in Spanish for Children and Adolescents

> California State University - San Marcos
> San Marcos, CA 92096-0001
> 760-750-4070; http://www.csusm.edu/campus_centers/csb

This Web site for Isabel Schon's Center for the Study of Books allows users to search for Spanish-language books by such criteria, or combination thereof, as: title, subject, grade/age, or publisher. According to Schon, all books listed are in print. The site also has links to pertinent workshops, conferences, and related organizations.

Diversity Tool Kit

http://projects.aclin.org/diversity

Now available online, this resource developed by the Colorado Council for Library Development's Committee on Library Services to Ethnic Populations includes a calendar of cultural events as well as a bibliography of resources related to the featured ethnic groups: African Americans, Native Americans, Asian Americans, and Hispanics.

Focus on Books: For School Library Media Centers, Spanish

Print version available from:
Los Angeles Unified School District, Library Services, Room 171
1320 West Third St.
Los Angeles, CA 90017
213-625-6486

This annual annotated list of new books put out by the Office of Instructional Media, is also available for purchase by other school districts to help with the selection of Spanish-language materials. Ten years' worth of the *Focus on Books* bibliographic records are available on CD-ROM from: SearchWare, P.O. Box 9182, Calabasas, CA 91372-9182; 1-800-243-2541.

Hispanic Outlook in Higher Education

Hispanic Outlook in Higher Education Publishing Co., Inc.
210 Route 4 East, Suite 310
Paramus, NJ 07652
http://www.HispanicOutlook.com

This bimonthly magazine is a good source of information for counselors who could help direct high school students to opportunities in colleges or universities. Each issue includes a column of seven or eight book reviews on subjects ranging from fiction to government policy to Latin American history to getting ahead in the business world. Video reviews are also included in some issues, and often one or two of the book or video reviews are for materials in Spanish. Materials reviewed are suitable for high school level or above.

The Horn Book Guide to Children's and Young Adult Books

> The Horn Book, Inc.
> 11 Beacon St., Suite 1000
> Boston, MA 02108
> http://www.hbook.com

> Issued twice per year, this book review magazine does re-view some Spanish-language books, although most of the re-views in the issues examined appeared to be for the K–3 level.

The Horn Book Magazine

> The Horn Book, Inc.
> 11 Beacon St., Suite 1000
> Boston, MA 02108
> http://www.hbook.com

> Though strong in the selection of multicultural books re-viewed, *The Horn Book* includes only a few reviews of Spanish-language or bilingual Spanish/English children's books.

> Related Web site:
> The Hornbook and Beyond: http://members.visi.net/~jfelker

Horning, Kathleen, Ginny Moore Kruse and Megan Schliesman. *CCBC Choices 1997*. Madison, Wisc.: Cooperative Children's Book Center, 1998.

> The Cooperative Children's Book Center at the University of Wisconsin-Madison reviews new children's and young-adult literature titles published in English, in an attempt to identify quality publications with multicultural themes. Some titles are bilingual in Spanish and English, making them suitable for speakers of both languages.

Kruse, Ginny Moore, Kathleen T. Horning and Megan Schliesman. *Multicultural Literature for Children and Young Adults: A Selected Listing of Books By and About People of Color. Vol. Two: 1991-1996*. Madison, Wisc.: Cooperative Children's Book Center, 1997.

> Most of the annotated listings in this volume first appeared in annual editions of *CCBC Choices*. Because it covers a period of six years, there are a number of bilingual titles included.

Library Journal

> 245 West 17th St.
> New York, NY 10011
> http://www.bookwire.com/

> Features a quarterly column of reviews of Spanish-language books.

MultiCultural Review: Dedicated to a Better Understanding of Ethnic, Racial and Religious Diversity

Greenwood Publishing Group
> P.O. Box 5007
> Westport, CT 06881-5007
> http://www.mcreview.com

> A quarterly publication that prints five to seven relevant articles per issue, plus reviews of multicultural materials. In a regular column, "Noteworthy Books in Spanish for Children and Adolescents," Isabel Schon reviews approximately 20 titles, materials that have been translated from English (i.e., Kipling, London, Stevenson) and materials that were originally written in Spanish. An occasional bilingual title will be reviewed in the main book review section.

Multilingual Computing

> 319 N. 1st Ave.
> Sandpoint, ID 83864
> 1-800-748-9824

> Although geared toward the businessperson, the articles, reviews, and advertisements could be helpful in identifying the latest software for a variety of languages and applications.

REFORMA Newsletter

c/o Rosario Garza, Bibliographical Center for Research
> 14394 E. Evans
> Aurora, CO 80014-1478

> This newsletter is distributed quarterly to members of Reforma: National Association to Promote Library Services to the Spanish-Speaking. A good selection of books, periodicals, and Web sites are reviewed each time.

School Library Journal

245 W. 17th St.
New York, NY 10011
http://www.bookwire.com/

Featured in the February, May, August, and November issues is the column, "Children's Books in Spanish," as well as advertisements for publishers and distributors of Spanish-language material. Each column features reviews of approximately 14 to 16 books, mostly suitable for children under junior high age. Occasionally there is a review for a bilingual title in another issue during the year.

■ Internet Resources

Leer

http://www.leer.nisc.com

A free electronic database for searching Spanish-language books, sponsored by National Information Services Corporation of Puerto Rico.

PLUS: Public Libraries Using Spanish

http://www.geocities.com/Athens/Thebes/8107

Tips on what other librarians have found successful with Spanish-speaking patrons; add your own ideas to this Web site.

Powerful Hispanic and Latin-American Images Revealed in Picture Books, compiled by Kay E. Vandergrift and Denise Agosto:

http://www.scils.rutgers.edu/special/kay/hispanic.html

This site provides a bibliography of picture books with positive depiction of Latino children.

Selecting Hispanic Books

http://falcon.jmu.edu/~ramseyil/mulhispbib.htm

A collection of bibliographies of children's books relating to Latin Americans, this site would be of value to librarians charged with materials selection.

Vangergrift's Children's Literature Page

http://www.scils.rutgers.edu/special/kay/childlit.html

> Gives a good overview of what constitutes good children's literature including illustrated materials about different ethnic groups; realistic, fanciful, regional, and historical fiction; biography; and poetry.

■ Listservs

Belonging to one or more of these Listservs, as well as ones set up for your particular state, can keep library staff up-to-date on issues, problems, solutions, and so forth in dealing with many library-related areas, including those related to serving speakers of other languages.

FORO-L Transborder Libraries Forum/Foro trinacional de bibliotecas

> A discussion forum for U.S., Mexican, and Canadian library staff. An unmoderated list; only those subscribed can participate.
> To subscribe send request to: requests@lists.gseis.ucla.edu
> Place this command in body of message: *subscribe FORO-L*

LM_NET

> International Listserv for "school library media people." Although not geared toward serving Spanish-speakers, many of the ideas are easily adaptable for all students.
> To subscribe, send an email message to: listserv@listserv.syr.edu
> Put nothing in the subject line, but write: *subscribe lm_net* and your name in the body of message.

MULTICULTURAL

> Participants in this list discuss children's and young-adult literature for and about all races and cultures.
> http://www.egroups.com/group/Multicultural
> Or write to: Multcultural-subscribe@onelist.com, leaving subject line and text empty.

PUBLIB

> As with LM_NET, this Listserv deals with public library services in general, but many of the ideas are easily adaptable for all categories of patrons.
> To subscribe, send email message: *SUB PubLib* plus your name to: listserv@sunsite.berkeley.edu

Reformanet

The electronic discussion group for REFORMA, the National Association to Promote Library Services to the Spanish-Speaking. Participants in the discussions need not be REFORMA members.

To subscribe send message to: listproc@lmrinet.ucsb.edu
Leave subject line blank.
In body of message type: subscribe reformanet [your name].
Delete any other words in message area.

■ Organizations

Center for the Study of Books in Spanish for Children and Adolescents
California State University
San Marcos, CA 92096-0001
760-750-4070
http://www.csusm.edu/campus_centers/csb/

The online Web page for Dr. Isabel Schon's Center offers a searchable database of over 5,000 in-print books in Spanish for children and young adults, as well as links to other pertinent sites. The Center also offers workshops, publications, and special activities for adults working with Latino children.

Center for Latin America
Center for Latin America
University of Wisconsin-Milwaukee
P.O. Box 413, Milwaukee, WI 53201
414-229-4401
http://www.uwm.edu/Dept/CLA

The Center receives funding from the U.S. Department of Education to support teaching, research, and outreach programs concerning Latin America.

Cooperative Children's Book Center (CCBC)
4290 Helen C. White Hall, University of Wisconsin-Madison
600 N. Park St., Madison, WI 53706-1403
608-262-4933
http://www.soemadison.wisc.edu/ccbc

CCBC is a "book examination center and research library" for children's and young-adult literature. As a division of the state university, its main audience is Wisconsin teachers, librarians, and students, but anyone working with children can benefit from its publications.

LARASA
Latin American Research and Service Agency
309 West First Ave.
Denver, CO 80223
303-722-5150

A research agency that publishes a monthly four-page report, *LARASA Report,* on topics (educational attainment, health issues, economics, etc.) of concern to Latinos in the United States. In English, it would be of interest to Latinos as well as others working with that population.

National Association for Bilingual Education (NABE)
1220 L St. NW, Suite 605
Washington, DC 20005-4018
202-898-1829
http://www.nabe.org

NABE is a professional organization addressing the educational needs of language-minority students in the United States, as well as promoting language competency and multicultural understanding.

National Clearinghouse for Bilingual Education (NCBE)The George Washington University Center for the Study of Language & Education
2011 Eye St. NW, Suite 200
Washington, D.C. 20006
202-467-0867; http://www.ncbe.gwu.edu

NCBE is funded by the U.S. Department of Education to collect and disseminate information about diverse learners in this country. The Online Library provides access to a number of relevant articles and other publications.

REFORMA: The National Association to Promote Library Services to the Spanish-Speaking
http://clnet.ucr.edu/library/reforma

Affiliated with the American Library Association, REFORMA seeks to promote library use among Latinos and the Spanish-speaking.

SALALM SecretariatBenson Latin American Collection
Sid Richardson Hall 1.109
The University of Texas at Austin
Austin, TX 78713-8916
http://libs.uga.edu/lais/laisintro.htm

SALALM = Seminar on the Acquisition of Latin American Library Materials. SALALM was formed as an international forum dealing with issues concerning the development of Spanish and Portuguese library collections in the United States as well as in the native countries.

■ Book Awards

The following are some of the awards given to Spanish-language and/or multicultural literature, for children as well as adults:

Americas Award for Children's and Young Adult Literature

http://www.uwm.edu/Dept/CLA/outreach_americas.html

An annual award given by CLASP (Consortium of Latin American Studies Programs at the Center for Latin America, University of Wisconsin-Milwaukee) to honor children's and young-adult books published in the United States in either English or Spanish that authentically portray experiences of Latinos in the United States, the Caribbean, or Latin America.

El Banco del Libro

http://public.csusm.edu/campus_centers/csb/english/lists

A Venezuelan organization that gives annual awards for children's literature. Its list of recommended books is available through the Web site of the Center for the Study of Books in Spanish for Children and Adolescents.

Barco de Vapor

An award from Spain for quality children's literature with humanitarian sentiments. A search of OCLC's First Search under *Barco de Vapor* will bring up titles that have received the award.

Hans Christian Andersen Awards

http://www.ibby.org

Every other year awards are given to a living author and illustrator who have made significant contributions to the international world of children's literature.

IBBY's Honour List

http://www.ibby.org

A biennial selection of outstanding children's literature titles which honors writers, illustrators and translators from IBBY member countries. The list of selected titles is available free of charge from IBBY.

Mildred L. Batchelder Award

Awarded annually by the American Library Association to the most outstanding children's book originally published in another country in a language other than English that was subsequently published in the United States.

Premio Alfaguara (Spain)

http://www.alfaguara.com

An annual international award for novels written Spanish, sponsored by Editorial Alfaguara, Madrid, Spain.

Premio Lazarillo (Spain)

An annual award to Spanish or Hispanic American writers and illustrators for the best children's or youth book. A search of *Premio Lazarillo* in First Search will list titles that have received the award.

Premio Literario Casa de las Américas

An annual award given since 1959 by the Havana, Cuba, publishing house. A few titles were retrieved when a search was done in First Search.

Pura Belpré Award

http://www.ala.org/alsc/belpre.html

A biennial award given by ALSC (Association for Library Service to Children) and REFORMA to honor Latino writers and illustrators for works dealing with the Latino cultural experience in the United States. The award is named for the first Latina librarian (a Puerto Rican) in the New York Public Library System.

Premios literarios en España (Literacy awards in Spain)

http://www.geocities.com/premiosliterarios

Although the text is in Spanish only, this site does list some of the more important literary awards in Spain.

■ Book Fairs

If your travel plans take you to one of these countries, perhaps you could arrange for your plans to coincide with one of these book fairs. A U.S. Library Events Calendar is available at: http://www.bookwire.com/ljdigital/calendar.htm.

Feria Internacional del Libro

Guadalajara, Jalisco, Mexico, November
Contact: David Unger, Division of Humanities NAC, 6293
The City College of New York, New York, NY 10031

The Spanish-language book fair to attend if at all possible, with publishers' representatives from throughout Latin America and the Spanish-speaking world. The American Library Association offers financial assistance and a number of U.S. librarians attend this fair each year.

International Book Fair

Palacio de Minería, Mexico City; March;
http://tolsa.mineria.unam.mx/esp/ferialib.htm

Self-proclaimed as "the event with most importance and tradition in Mexico City," this book fair is organized by The National Autonomous University of Mexico.

Feria Internacional del Libro

P.O. Box 9066272
San Juan, Puerto Rico 00906-6272
787-721-0844;
email: feriapr@caribe.net; mid-November

Includes cultural and social activities along with special programs for book and information professionals.

■ Conferences/Workshops

American Library Association Annual Convention

State Library Association Conventions: Browse vendor displays and look for relevant member sessions.

BUENO Center for Multicultural Education
   School of Education, Campus
   Box 249, University of Colorado
   Boulder, CO 80309-0249
   303-492-5416
   http://www.colorado.edu/education/BUENO

   Holds institutes each summer dealing with issues of bilingual, multicultural, and special education.

California Association for Bilingual Education
   660 South Figueroa St., Suite 1040
   Los Angeles, CA 90017
   213-532-3850

   Annual conference held in late fall; free and open to the public. Literary activities for children and adults with opportunities to purchase materials from vendors.

Center for the Study of Books in Spanish for Children and Adolescents
   California State University
   San Marcos, CA 92096-0001
   760-750-4070
   http://www.csusm.edu/campus_centers/csb

   Holds summer workshops on various aspects of Spanish-language children's literature.

National Association for Bilingual Education
   1220 L St. NW, Suite 605
   Washington, D.C. 20005-4018
   202-898-1829
   http://www.nabe.org

   Annual conference: a great opportunity to hear challenging speakers and to network with others serving bilingual children.

Seminar on the Acquisition of Latin American Library Materials (SALALM)
   SALALM Secretariat, Benson Latin American Collection, Sid Richardson Hall 1.109
   The University of Texas at Austin
   Austin, TX 78713-8916
   http://libs.uga.edu/lais/laisintro.htm

An international forum dealing with issues concerning the development of Spanish and Portuguese bibliographic information and library collections in the United States as well as in the native countries. An annual conference is held each spring.

Transborder Library Forum=*Foro Transfronterizo de Bibliotecas*
http://www.mxl.cetys.mx/foro

An annual conference for librarians, held in March, alternating locations between Mexico and the border regions of the United States. Information about date and place first appears on the FORO listserv.

Trejo-Foster Foundation: National Institute for Hispanic Library Education

Occurs every other year; look for notice of future institutes on *Reformanet*. The 1999 conference, held at the University of South Florida in Tampa had as its theme: "Library Services to Youth of Hispanic Heritage."

Appendix B
Vocabulary, Examples, and Forms/
Vocabulario, Ejemplos, y Formularios

English/Inglés	Spanish/Español	English/Inglés	Spanish/Español
Adolescents	los Adolescentes	Book cover	la Portada del libro
Adults	los Adultos	Bookmark	el Marcador de libros
Alphabet	el Alfabeto	Bookmobile	el Bibliobús
Alphabet (book)	el Abecedario	Bookshelf/Case	el Estante para libros
Almanac	el Almanaque	Bookstore	la Librería
Article (Magazine)	el Artículo de Revista	Book Spine	el Lomo del libro
Assignment / Report	el Trabajo / el Informe	To borrow	Tomar prestado
Atlas	el Atlas	By (as in, this book is by ..)	Por
Author	el Autor	Call number	el Número de clasificación
Autobiography	la Autobiografía	Card catalog	el Catálogo de tarjetas
Bathroom	el Baño / el Servicio sanitario	Cartoons	las Caricaturas
Biography	la Biografía	Cassette	el Cassette
Biweekly	Catorcenal; quincenal	Chapter	el Capítulo
Book	el Libro	Chart	el Gráfico

English/Inglés	Spanish/Español	English/Inglés	Spanish/Español
Check out books here	Registre los libros que se llevan aquí	Hard cover	la Tapa dura
Child; children	el Niño, la niña; los niños	Heading	el Encabezamiento
Children's room	la Sala infantil	Hispanic American	Hispanoestadouni-dense (Literally: Hispanic United Statesan)
Circulation desk	el Registro	Information	la Información
Comic strips	las Tiras cómicas	Interlibrary Loan	el Préstamo interbibliotecario
Cover, Book jacket	la Cubierta	Juvenile	Juvenil
Dictionary	el Diccionario	Keyword	la Palabra clave
Distance education	la Educación a distancia	Learning Resources Center (LRC)	el Centro de Recursos del Aprendizaje (CRA)
Distributor	la Distribuidora	Librarian	la (el) Bibliotecaria(o)
Easy book	el Libro de lectura fácil	Library Science	la Bibliotecnología
Encyclopedia	la Enciclopedia	Library Staff	los Asistentes de biblioteca
Exit / Entrance	la Salida / la Entrada	Literary Circle	la Tertulia literaria
Fiction/Novel	la Ficción/la Novela	Magazine	la Revista
Fine (for late return)	la Multa	Map	el Mapa (irregular - it is a masculine noun even though it ends in "a")
Good afternoon	Buenas tardes	Microfiche	las Microfichas transparentes
Good day, Good morning, Hello	Buenos días	Microfilm	La Micropelícula
Good night	Buenas noches	News	las Noticias

English/Inglés	Spanish/Español	English/Inglés	Spanish/Español
Newspaper	el Periódico	Reference Room	la Sala de consulta
Nonfiction	la Literatura no novelesca/ No-Ficción	Sports	los Deportes
Online catalog	el Catálogo electrónico	Subscription	la Suscripción
Page	la Página	Subject	el Tema (another irregular noun that is masculine even though it ends in "a")
Pamphlet	el Pamfleto	Subtitle	el Subtítulo
Picture Book	el Libro de dibujos /el Libro ilustrado	Thank you	Gracias
Picture File	el Archivo de retratos	Title	el Título
Please	Por favor	User, Patron	el Usuario
Pocket Books	los Libros de Bolsillo	Vertical File	el Archivo vertical
Poem/ Poetry	el Poema / la Poesía	Verso	Verso
Preschool book	el Libro infantil	Welcome	Bienvenido
Reference Book	el Libro de Consulta / de Referencias	Young-Adult Fiction	la Ficción para jóvenes
Reference Librarian	el (la) Bibliotecario (a) de consulta	Young People	la Gente joven; jóvenes
		You're welcome	No tiene porqué; no hay de qué

Library Phrases/Las Frases Bibliotecarias

English/Inglés	Spanish/Español
All rights reserved	Todos los derechos reservados
Don't run	No corra
How may I help you?	¿Cómo le puedo ayudar?
Just a minute, please	Un momento, por favor (an especially good phrase for a non-Spanish speaking staff members to know when they need to get another person to help a patron over the telephone)
Once upon a time	Había una vez
To renew a book	Renovar un libro
To reserve a book	Reservar un libro
Return books here	Devolución de libros – Aquí
Speak softly, please	Por favor, hable suave; OR: Hable con voz baja, por favor.
What do you need?	¿Qué necesita usted?
What is your subject?	¿Cuál es su tema?
Theme, assignment, report	Tema, tarea, informe
Do you have a library pass?	¿Tiene el permiso para ir /venir a la biblioteca? (Do you have permission to go/come to the library?)
What time do you need to return to class?	¿A qué hora debe regresar usted a la clase?
You may borrow this book for ___weeks (days), then you must return it.	Usted puede tomar prestado este libro por____ semanas (días), y entonces debe devolverlo.

Spanish Computer Vocabulary
Vocabulario de la Computadora

English/Inglés	Spanish/Español	English/Inglés	Spanish/Español
To go back	Regresar	E-mail	E-mail
Button	el Botón	Enter words to search	Ingrese palabras a buscar
To cancel	Cancelar	To erase	Borrar
Click	Pulse, Seleccione, Pinche, Haga un click	File (n)	el Archivo
To close	Cerrar	To find	Encontrar
Compact disc	el Disco compacto	Folder	el Fólder
Computer	la Computadora	To go forward	Seguir/Continuar
Computer disk	el Disco de la computadora	Font	la Letra
To copy	Copiar	Game	el Juego
Cursor	el Cursor	To go	Ir
To cut	Cortar	Hard drive	el Disco duro
Cybernetic	Cibernético	Help	Ayuda, apoyo
To delete	Borrar	Home	Home
To digitize	Digitalizar	Home page	la Página hogar
Directory	el Directorio	Ink cartridge	el Cartucho de tinta
To edit	Editar	Inkjet	la Inyectora de tinta
Electronic mail	el Correo electrónico; el Buzón electrónico	Key (of a keyboard)	la Tecla
Electronic network	la Red electrónica	Keyboard	el Teclado

English/Inglés	Spanish/Español	English/Inglés	Spanish/Español
Mail	el Correo	Screen	la Pantalla
Mailbox	el Buzón	To search (v)	Buscar
Memory	la Memoria	Search (n)	la Búsqueda
Menu	el Menú	Search engine	el Buscador
Mouse	el Ratón	To select	Seleccionar
Mouse pad	la Alfombrilla para ratón	Server	el Servidor
To move	Mover	Size	el Tamaño
Online	En línea	Software	el Software
To open	Abrir	Sound card	la Tarjeta de sonido
Operating system	el Sistema operativo	Speaker	el Parlante
Options	las Opciones	To stop	Parar
Paper	el Papel	Trash(can)	el Basurero
To paste	Pegar	Trash (v)	Botar
To print	Imprimir	To view	Ver
Printer	la Impresora	Virtual reality	la Realidad virtual
Processor	el Procesador	WWW	WWW
Program	el Programa	Web page, Web site	la Página Web
To quit	Salir	Window	la Ventana, la Vitrina
To save	Salvar		

How to Care for Your Library Books
Como Cuidar Los Libros De Biblioteca

English/Inglés	Spanish/Español
Don't get them wet.	No los traiga mojados.
Don't write in them.	No los raye.
Don't tear the pages.	No arranque las páginas.
Don't let your dog chew on them.	No se los dé al perro como comida.
Don't fold the pages over; use a bookmark.	No doble las páginas; use un marcador de libros.
Keep them out of the reach of small children.	Déjelos fuera del alcance de los niños.
Keep them clean.	Manténgalos limpios.
Return them on time or renew them.	Devuélvalos a tiempo o renuévelos.
Don't lend them to anyone else.	No se los preste a nadie más.
If you do not return the books, you will have to pay the replacement cost of each.	Si usted no los regresa, deberá pagar el costo completo de cada libro.

Title Page/Portada

La educación de los Aztecas:	Title/ Título
cómo se formó el carácter del pueblo mexica	Subtitle/Sub-título
Fernando *Díaz* Infante	Author/Autor Alphabetize under the paternal last name of Díaz
Panorama Editorial, S.A. de	Publisher/Casa Editorial S. A. = Sociedad Anónima = Limited
C.V.	C.V. = Capital Variable, a legal standing for businesses Cia. = abbreviation for Compañía (not present here)

Verso/Verso

LA EDUCACION DE LOS AZTECAS	Title/Título
Portada:	Cover:
Dibujo: Heraclio Ramírez	Drawing:
Ilustraciones:	Illustrations:
Fernando Díaz Infante	
Primera edición: 1992	First edition:
Primera reimpresión: 1993	First reprint:
© Panorama Editorial, S.A. de C.V.	
Manuel Ma.Contreras 45-B	Street Address/*Dirección* [notice that the street number comes after the street name, and may sometimes be followed by the neighborhood (*colonia*) name; *Ma.* is an abbreviation for the name *María.*]
Col. San Rafael	
06470 México, D. F.	Zip Code/Código postal [comes before city name, México (City), not to be confused with the name of the country]. D. F. = *Distrito Federal*, meaning the Federal District of Mexico City
Impreso en México	Printed in Mexico
ISBN 968-38-0305-9	

**(Permission to reproduce the title page and verso was given by
Luis Castañeda of Panorama Editorial.)**

OnLine Catalog Example
Ejemplo Del Catálogo Electrónico

AUTHOR (s)/ AUTOR (es)	Díaz Infante, Fernando
TITLE (s)/ TITULO (s)	La educación de los Aztecas : cómo se formó el carácter del pueblo mexica / Fernando Díaz Infante.
	Mexico City : Panorama Editorial, 1992.
	144 p.: ill.; 20 cm.
OTHER ENTRIES/ TEMAS (MATERIA):	Mexico History to 1519
	México Historia hasta 1519
	Aztecs
	Aztecas
LOCN: LEADVL	STATUS: Not checked out —
LOCALIDAD:	ESTADO:
CALL #: F1219 .D52 1992	
NUMERO DE CLASIFICACION:	

Dewey Decimal System
Clave De Localización

000-099   **General Works/Generalidades**

100-199   **Philosophy/Filosofía**

200-299   **Religion/Religión**

300-399   **Sociology/Ciencias sociales:**
               Economics, Law/Economía, Derecho,
               Education/Educación

400-499   **Language/Lenguas**

500-599   **Science/Ciencias puras:**
               Mathematics/Matemáticas,
               Physics, Chemistry/Física, Química,
               Biology/Biología

600-699   **Useful Arts/Ciencias aplicadas:**
               Medicine/Medicina,
               Engineering/Ingeniería,
               Agriculture/Agricultura

700-799   **Fine Arts/Bellas Artes:**
               Architecture/Arquitectura,
               Painting, Music/Pintura, Música
               Photography/Fotografía

800-899   **Literature/Literatura:**
               Poetry, Theater/Poesía, Teatro,
               Essay/Ensayo

900-999   **History, Travel/Historia, Geografía**
               Fiction/Ficción
               Biography/Biografía

Sample Registration Forms

Colorado Mountain College Learning Resources Center
(Biblioteca)
Borrower Registration Form/Forma de Inscribirse

Today's Date/Fecha: _____

Check One: CMC Student _____ Staff_____Faculty_____ Community____
           Estudiante   Empleado   Facultad   Comunidad

Name/Nombre_____
            Last/Apellido   First/Primer Nombre

If you are a CMC student, please give us your Social Security Number: _____

Si usted es estudiante de CMC, favor de indicar su Número de Seguro Social:

_____

Current Mailing Address/Dirección donde recibe correspondencia:

   Street/PO Box/ Apt. #/Dorm #: _____

   Calle/ Apartado/Número de Apartamento:

   City/Ciudad: _____

   State/Estado: _____ Zip Code/Código Postal: _____

   Telephone Number/Número de Teléfono:_____

IF YOU ARE A CMC STUDENT, give us a permanent address where you can always be reached; for example, your parents' address:

SI USTED ES ESTUDIANTE DE CMC, favor de escribir su dirección permanente; por ejemplo, la dirección de sus padres:

   Street/PO Box/Apt.#/Dorm #: _____

   Calle/Apartado/Número de Apartamento:

   City/Ciudad: _____

   State/Estado: _____ Zip Code/Código Postal: _____

Telephone Number / Número de Teléfono _____

* *

TIMBERLINE CAMPUS

901 South Highway 24, Leadville, Colorado 80461 719-486-4250

BIBLIOTECA PUBLICA
DE LAKE COUNTY

Número _____ REGISTRO DE PRESTATARIO Expirará _____

Nombre completo _____

Dirección de habitación _____

Dirección donde recibe su correo _____

Leadville, CO 80461 o _____ Número de teléfono _____

Prueba de dirección _____

Registro temporal_____ Fecha de nacimiento _____

Yo pido el privilegio de pedir prestado libros de la biblioteca pública de Lake County. Prometo ser responsable de todos los materiales prestados a cuenta de mi tarjeta, de dar noticia puntual de cambio de nombre, dirección, número de teléfono y de obedecer todas las reglas de la biblioteca. Edad si menos de 18 _____ Firma (de padres) _____

LAKE COUNTY PUBLIC LIBRARY

Number _____ BORROWER REGISTRATION Expires _____

Name _____
             Last   First   Middle

Street Address _____

Mailing Address (if different) _____

Leadville, CO 80461 or _____Phone _____

Proof of residency _____

Date of Birth _____

I agree to observe all rules and regulations of the Lake County Public Library and to give immediate notice of any change of name, address or phone number.
Age if under 18 _____ (Parent's) Signature _____

Sample Parent Letter

Lake County Public Library
1115 Harrison Ave.
Leadville, Colorado 80461-3398
(719) 486-0569
FAX (719) 486-3544

Estimados padres:

Nosotros aquí en la Biblioteca Pública de Lake County estamos muy contentos de que la maestra de su hijo vaya a traer su clase a la Biblioteca cada dos semanas para escuchar cuentos y para sacar prestado hasta tres libros con cada visita durante el año escolar.

Los jóvenes pueden llevar los libros a su clase para compartir conotros, o a su casa si la maestra lo permite.

Para tener en cuenta los centenares de libros prestados por semana, tarjetas amarillas de registro fueron enviadas a su casa al comienzo del año escolar para que usted pudiera llenarlas y firmarlas. Su firma indica que su niño tiene su permiso de sacar prestado libros de la Biblioteca Pública cuando venga solo o con su clase, que usted será responsable por libros perdidos o dañados, que usted ayudará a devolver los libros a tiempo y que nos informará de qualquier cambio de dirección o número de teléfono.

Al recibir las tarjetas amarillas de registración completadas, se la daremos una tarjeta azul a su hijo. La bibiotecaria de niños mantendrá estas tarjetas y se las entregará con cada visita escolar. Si su hijo visita la Biblioteca Pública solo, o acompañado de un adulto, todavía puede sacar prestado libros sin su tarjeta azul, ya que nosotros tendremos las tarjetas amarillas en nuestro archivo.

¡Muchas gracias por su deseo de participar!

BIBLIOTECA PÚBLICA DE LAKE COUNTY

Lake County Public Library
1115 Harrison Ave.
Leadville, Colorado 80461-3398
(719) 486-0569
Fax (719) 486-3544

Dear Parents:

We at the Lake County Public Library are very pleased that your child's teacher has decided to bring the class to the Public Library for a period of story-telling and book selection every two weeks during the school year.

We encourage your child to borrow up to three books each time the class visits and to take the books back to the classroom to read and share with other children, or to take home if the teacher allows.

In order for us to keep track of the hundreds of books the children check out each week, yellow registration cards were sent home at the beginning of the school year to be filled out and signed by you. Your signature indicates the child has your permission to borrow books from the Public Library either on his/her own or when the class visits, and that you will be responsible for any loss or dam-age, for helping to see that books are returned on time, and for informing us of any address or phone number changes.

Once we have received the yellow registration card accurately filled in, we issue a blue Library ID card to each child. The Children's Librarian keeps these cards and passes them out at each class visit. If your child visits the Public Li-brary either on his/her own or accompanied by an adult, s/he is still entitled to borrow books even without a blue ID card since we will have the yellow registra-tion card on file.

Thank you for your willingness to participate!

LAKE COUNTY PUBLIC LIBRARY

El Cuestionario Bibliotecario

Biblioteca _____ Fecha _____

Gracias por su visita a la Biblioteca Pública de la Ciudad de Salt Lake

Favor de marcar el cuadro que identifique el propósito de su visita hoy.

1. Vine a la biblioteca para:
    a.   ___ Encontrar información específica
    b.   ___ Buscar los siguientes materiales:
        c.   ___ libros
        d.   ___ casetes
        e.   ___ discos compactos
        f.   ___ periódicos/revistas
        g.   ___ videos
    h.   ___ Ojear la colección en general
    i.   ___ Usar el Internet
    j.   ___ Estudiar, solo o en grupo
    k.   ___ Atender a una junta, un programa, or una exhibición
    l.   ___ Usar la copiadora
    m.   ___ Otro propósito: _____

2. Estaba buscando materiales
    n.   ___ Escritos/interpretados por algún autor o artista
    o.   ___ De un título específico
    p.   ___ Sobre un tema
    q.   ___ Otro propósito: _____

3. Encontré los materiales que necesitaba: r. ___Sí s. ___No t. ___Algunos

4. No pude encontrar los materiales que necesitaba, y tuve que:
    u.   ___ Pedir auyda de un bibliotecario(a)
    v.   ___ Pedir que algún título sea reservado para mí
    w.   ___ Pedir que materiales sean mandados de otra biblioteca
    x.   ___ Buscar otros materiales
    y.   ___ Dejé de buscar y me fui sin nada
    z.   ___ Otro: _____

5. Los materiales que necesitaba, pero que no encontré, están escritos abajo: _____

6. El código postal de mi domicilio es: _____
Le invitamos que nos deje cualquier comentario: _____

_____

_____

_____

_____

(Favor de usar el otro lado de esta página si necesita más espacio para su comentario)

Library Survey

Agency _____ Date _____

Thank you for visiting the Salt Lake City Public Library

Please mark the box that correctly identifies the purpose of your visit today.

1. I came to the library to:

    a.   ____ Look for particular information

    b.   ____ Look for particular library materials (please specify)

        c.   ____ books

        d.   ____ cassettes

        e.   ____ compact discs

        f.   ____ newspapers/magazines

        g.   ____ videos

    h.   ____ Browse, nothing particular in mind

    i.   ____ Use the Internet

    j.   ____ Study, alone or in a group

    k.   ____ Attend a meeting, program or exhibit

    l.   ____ Use the photocopy machine

    m.   ____ Other _____ _____

2. I was looking for materials:

    n.   ____ Written/performed by a particular author or artist

    o.   ____ With a particular title

    p.   ____ On a particular subject

    q.   ____ Other _____

3. I found the materials I needed: r. ___ Yes s. ___ No t. ___ Some

4. I could not find the material I needed, so I:

    u.   ____ Asked a librarian for help

    v.   ____ Asked for the material to be placed on hold for me

    w.   ____ Asked for the material to be transferred from another library

    x.   ____ Looked for something else

    y.   ____ Gave up and left without anything

    z.   ____ Other _____

5. The material I needed, but could not find, is listed below:

_____
_____
_____
_____

6. My home zip code is: _____

We welcome any comments you would like to make.

_____
_____
_____
_____

(Forms created by Ben Ocón and Juan Tomás Lee. Permission to reprint granted by Salt Lake City Public Library.)

Appendix C
Publishers and Distributors

D = Distributor, P = Publisher

AA Music Enterprises - D
2137 E. 37th St.
Vernon, CA 90058
1-800-797-1999

Offers a wide selection of CDs and cassette tapes for regional Mexican, Rock, Latin Pop/Dance, and Tejano music.

Aims International Books, Inc. - D
7709 Hamilton Ave.
Cincinnati, Ohio 45231-3103
1-800-733-2067
http://www.aimsbooks.com

Although Aims distributes books in several languages, its most extensive collection seems to be Spanish-language material for children from preschool to young-adult ages. In addition to books, Aims offers stickers, posters, maps, and charts in Spanish.

Alta Book Center - D
14 Adrian Ct.
Burlingame, CA 94010
1-800-258-2375
http://www.altaesl.com

Self-proclaimed as the "largest source of ESL books and materials in the world," this company also has bilingual Spanish/English books, CD-ROMs, and cassette tapes.

Los Andes Publishing, Inc. - D

P.O. Box 2344
La Puente, CA 91746
1-800-532-8872
http://www.losandes.com

Areas covered include: literature for pre-kindergarten to sixth grade and up, materials relating to curriculum areas, computer software, and CD-ROMs such as *Larousse Visual Diccionario Multimedia* and *Larousse Enciclopedia Básica Multimedia*. Los Andes is a U.S. supplier for Grupo Anaya, a major publisher from Spain whose catalog includes some well-known software packages in Spanish. It also distributes materials from Plaza y Janés. Examination copies for some materials can be arranged.

Arcoiris Records, Inc.

P.O. Box 7428
Berkeley, CA 94707
510-527-5539
Fax: 510-526-8555
http://www.joseluisorozco.com

Children's music of Latin America recorded on audiocassettes and CDs by José-Luis Orozco.

Arte Público Press - P

University of Houston, 4800 Calhoun
Houston, Texas 77204-2090
http://bentley.uh.edu/arte_publico

Self-proclaimed as the "oldest and largest publisher of U.S. Hispanic literature," Arte Público publishes English and bilingual books for older teens and adults, although its imprint, Piñata Books, publishes literary materials for children. This publisher does not arrange for Spanish translations, but does publish translations that the author can secure.

Asia for Kids - D

Master Communications, Inc., 4480
Lake Forest Dr., Suite 302, Cincinnati, OH 45242-3726
513-563-3100
http://www.afk.com

Although emphasizing Asian-language materials for younger children, Asia for Kids does have some Spanish-language resources for children, as well as helps for adults working with these LEP students. Included among the book titles are a couple of bilingual picture dictionaries.

Astran, Inc. - D
591 S. W. 8th St.
Miami, FL 33130
305-858-4300
http://www.astranbooks.com

Astran's catalog lists Spanish-language titles by subject with an English translation. The majority of titles are for adults, with a limited number for children. Books are mainly imports from Spain, Mexico, and Argentina, but no publishers are listed. A listing of best-sellers is available on the Web site.

Audio Buff Co., Inc. - D
P.O. Box 2628
Athens, OH 45701-5428
740-593-3014

A large selection of Latino music, foreign language, and children's recordings in CD, laser disc, audio- and videocassette formats. No minimum order requirement.

Audio-Forum: The Language Source - D
96 Broad St.
Guilford, CT 06437
1-800-243-1234
http://agoralang.com/audioforum.html

Audio-Forum offers audiovisual materials in approximately 100 languages, and although they are geared toward people learning those languages, some of the more advanced materials might be suitable for native speakers. Included in the catalog are games such as Monopoly® and Scrabble® in Spanish, CD-ROM programs, recorded ethnic music, and foreign films.

Baker & Taylor - D
National Sales Headquarters
5 Lakepointe Plaza, Suite 500
2709 Water Ridge Pkwy
Charlotte, NC 28217
1-800-775-1800
http://www.baker-taylor.com

Check Web site for desired Spanish-language titles. If that is not satisfactory, speak with a customer service representative.

Bilingual Books, Inc. - P
511 Eastlake Avenue E.
Seattle, WA 98109
1-800-488-5068

Publishes materials for learners of French, Italian, German, and Spanish.

Bilingual Educational Services, Inc.- D
2514 South Grand Ave.
Los Angeles, CA 90007-9979
1-800-448-6032
http://www.besbooks.com

BES materials are especially geared to support classrooms and school libraries with Spanish-speaking students, but a public library could also find the selections useful. Catalog entries are grouped by age level, with brief annotations about subject or theme. Several *Time-Life* series in Spanish are available, as well as textbooks, CD-ROMs, and A-V materials. Cataloging is available for online circulation systems; soft-cover books have been rebound to be more durable.

Bilingual Publications Company - D
270 Lafayette St.
New York, NY 10012
212-431-3500

Bilingual Publications Company carries children's and adult books published in Spain, Latin America, and the United States. In particular, it has books from Plaza y Janés, a major publisher in Spain that is distributed in this country through Bantam Doubleday Dell. Bilingual Publications offers an approval plan for Spanish-language books, based on a profile of library's particular needs. Books that do not meet the library's needs may be returned.

The Bookmen Inc. - D
525 North Third St.
Minneapolis, MN 55401
1-800-328-8411

The Bookmen offers a selection of Spanish-language and bilingual books for preschoolers through adults. Among the popular series it carries are: *Berenstain Bears, Little House on the Prairie,* and *Magic School Bus*, as well as titles by R. L. Stein and Beverly Cleary. Discounts offered to libraries.

Britannica, Inc.- P
310 South Michigan Ave.
Chicago, IL 60604-4293
1-800-621-3900
http://www.eb.com

Britannica offers two Spanish-language encyclopedias: the 18-volume *Enciclopedia Hispánica* and the four-volume *Lexipedia*.

C. D. Stampley Enterprises, Inc. - D
P.O. Box 33172
Charlotte, NC 28233
704-333-6631

Stampley has the Launch Pad Library and *National Geographic* series in Spanish as well as *Biblioteca de Descubrimientos,* a 12-volume set for children aged 6 to 12 on different topics about the world and life.

Capstone Press
P.O. Box 669
Mankato, MN 56002-0669
1-800-747-4992
http://www.capstone-press.com

Capstone has a wide range of High Interest/Low Reading Level books, including some titles that have been translated into Spanish.

Center for Latin America, University of Wisconsin-Milwaukee, Videotape Special Collection;
http://www.uwm.edu:80/Dept/CLA/video.html

Listed on the Web page are English, Spanish, Portuguese, and/or bilingual videotapes that can be rented or purchased, dealing with history and social conditions of various Latin American countries.

Central Valley Video Distributors-D
910 W. Yosemite Ave.
Madera, CA 93637
559-675-6827

Distributes a number of adult and children's video titles, some of which are subtitled and others dubbed in Spanish. The selection includes popular titles (such as *101 Dalmations*), classics (*Peter Pan*), classic Mexican artists, rodeo shows, and religious themes.

Charlesbridge Publishing - P
85 Main St.
Watertown, MA 02472
1-800-225-3214
http://www.charlesbridge.com

Charlesbridge has a series of ESL and bilingual children's books, including the culturally sensitive works of Nancy Tabor (see Chapter 3).

Chelsea House Publishers - P
P.O. Box 914
Broomall, PA 19008-0914
1-800-848-BOOK
http://www.chelseahouse.com

The Chelsea House Spanish-Language and Hispanic Studies collection has series of books in Spanish on the Earth, Plants, and the Senses, plus a video series on famous Hispanics. The volumes may be purchased separately or as a set.

Children's Book Press - P
246 First St., Suite 101
San Francisco, CA 94105
415-995-2200

Specializing in multicultural children's literature, Children's Book Press has several titles that are bilingual in English and Spanish.

Children's Press - P
A Grolier Publishing Company
90 Sherman Turnpike
Danbury, CT 06819

Has a few sets of books in Spanish in the science and social studies areas for early elementary-age students. Cataloging is available.

Chulainn Publishing Corp. - D
244 Wagon Tongue Rd.
Bailey, CO 80421
1-888-525-2665
http://www.newpublications.com

Chulainn's Web site provides links to five Spanish-language publishers as well as a version of Spanish Books in Print, from which selections can be made. Print catalog is arranged under the following subjects: fiction, Mexican themes, self-help, reference and hobbies, poetry and prose, health, computers, and children's and young-adult. Discounts given on orders over $100.00.

Cinco Puntos Press - P

2709 Louisville
El Paso, TX 79930
915-566-9072

Cinco Puntos is the publisher of well-known storyteller, Joe Hayes, many of whose works are available in bilingual versions in book and audiocassette tape formats.

Círculo de Lectores:

http://www.circulolectores.com

A Spanish-language book club for readers in the United States. An interesting feature on the Web site are brief biographies of the featured U.S. and Latino authors—similar to the *Contemporary Authors* series.

Columbia House - D

Club Música Latina
1400 North Fruitridge Ave.
Terre Haute, IN 47812-9011
http://www.columbiahouse.com/music

Columbia House's Club Música Latina offers a monthly selection of CDs of Latino music. As with any record club, after the purchase of a specified number of CDs, you can purchase as few or as many as you can afford.

Computadora Fácil

150 S. Glenoaks Blvd, #8056
Burbank, CA 91502
818-243-0087
http://www.computadorafacil.com

This company has videotapes that teach beginning to intermediate computer and software skills to Spanish speakers.

Continental Book Company - D

Western Division
625 E. 70th Ave., #5
Denver, CO 80229
303-289-1761

Eastern Division
80-00 Cooper Ave., #29
Glendale, NY 11385
718-326-0560
http://www.continentalbook.com

Offers a wide range of Spanish, bilingual, and ESL materials for children through adults in the following formats: books, periodicals, audio- and videocassettes, textbooks, computer software, maps, games, posters, and reference materials. Continental is a good source of selections for a beginning collection to serve Spanish-speakers.

Coral Communications Group, LLC - D

880 Fifth Ave., 8th Floor
New York NY 10021
212-744-7090

Offers audio books in Spanish primarily for adults, although a few titles would be appropriate for children.

Dearborn Financial Publishing, Inc. - P

155 North Wacker Dr.
Chicago, IL 60606-1719
312-836-4400
http://www.dearborn.com

Dearborn publishes several titles about business and real estate in Spanish.

Del Sol Books, Inc. -D

29257 Bassett Rd.
Westlake, OH 44145
1-888-335-7651

Del Sol can provide a catalog of books written or translated by Alma Flor Ada, as well as material by others who are respected in the field of bilingual materials for Latino children such as F. Isabel Campoy, Pat Mora, Suni Paz, and Gary Soto. The company also offers audiocassette tapes of music and stories.

Donars Spanish Books - D

P.O. Box 808
Lafayette, CO 80026
1-800-552-3316

Donars publishes a monthly, annotated list of books they have available for children and adults. Is a distributor for Plaza & Janés.

El Dorado Books - D

4225 W. Glendale Ave., Suite A-2
Phoenix, AZ 85051
1-800-615-4614
http://www.eldoradobooks.com

Features bilingual and Spanish-language materials for children from preschool through high school. Reference materials include dictionaries, thesauri, atlases, and computer software. Student encyclopedias include: *Larousse Enciclopedia de Niños*; *Enciclopedia Ilustrada de los Niños* (Ediciones Monte Verde); *Enciclopedia "Me Pregunto Por Qué"* (Everest); and *Enciclopedia de Ecología* (SM).

Downtown Book Center, Inc. - D

247 SE First St.
Miami, FL 33131
1-800-599-8712
http://www.libros-direct.com

Sells popular titles from many Spanish-language publishers. Services offered include approval plan, book processing, and discount for libraries.

Econo-Clad Books - D

P.O. Box 1777
Topeka, KS 66601
1-800-255-3502
http://sagebrushcorp.com/redirect.efn

Offers a number of bilingual and Spanish titles for primary through secondary grades. Prebinding and cataloging are available for titles offered.

Ediciones Ekaré - P

Florida Representative: Alejandra Dearden; 1-813-250-1238

Ekaré is a respected Venezuelan publisher of children's books, with a warehouse in New York. A bilingual catalog of books is available from the U.S. representative.

EDMARK

P.O. Box 97021
Redmond, WA 98073-9721
1-800-362-2890
http://www.edmark.com

EDMARK has four instructional software programs in Castilian Spanish for pre-kindergarten through second grade. It also offers other computer resources for older students of English and Spanish.

Educational Publishers - D

3402 Burson Rd.
Valley Springs, CA 95252
209-772-9431

This distributor handles Spanish-language books for children through adults from Grupo Editorial Norma, Santillana USA, and Fernández USA, as well as titles in English.

Educational Record Center, Inc. - D

3233 Burnt Mill Dr. Suite 100
Wilmington, NC 28403-2698
1-800-438-1637

Selections include Spanish read-along tape and book sets, plus bilingual music audiocassettes and videos.

Emblem Interactive, Inc.

1400 S.W. First St.
Miami, FL 33135
305-649-1207
http://www.embleminteractive.com

Offers a number of Spanish-language, educational, interactive software programs, most suitable for older elementary through adult.

FDC Publishing Corp. - D

939 Crandon Blvd.
Key Biscayne, FL 33149
1-800-407-4770

Planeta, a major publisher from Spain, is distributed exclusively in the United States by FDC. Among other things, Planeta has *Libros de Bolsillo* (pocket books) and multimedia computer software including: *Enciclopedia Multimedia, Gran Diccionario Enciclopédico,* and *Atlas Mundial Interactiva.*

Facets Video - D
 1517 W. Fullerton Ave.
 Chicago, IL 60614
 1-800-331-6197
 http://www.facets.org

 Facets carries Spanish and Latin American films for adults or older teens on video, laser disc, and DVD. Films may be purchased or rented.

Farrar, Straus, Giroux - P
 19 Union Square West
 New York, NY 10003
 212-741-6900

 The Mirasol/*libros juveniles* imprint of this publisher includes several Spanish translations of favorite children's books.

Fernández USA Publishing Co. - P
 1210 East 223rd St. Suite 309
 Carson, CA 90745-9980

 The selections in the Fernández USA catalog would be good for a school library to have to supplement the curriculum from K–12. Besides books, teaching charts, anatomical models, and wall maps, the CD-ROM *Diccionario Academia Enciclopédico* is available in Spanish. Cataloging for online systems is available. These materials are also distributed by several suppliers listed later.

Fiesta Book Company - D
 P.O. Box 490641
 Key Biscayne, FL 33149-0641
 1-305-858-4843

 Has a number of fiction and nonfiction titles, mainly for older students and adults, including special packages and volume discounts. Although the physical quality was not examined, this would be a good source for inexpensive books for special giveaways or incentives.

Films for the Humanities & Sciences - D

P.O. Box 2053
Princeton, NJ 08543-2053
1-800-257-5126
http://www.films.com

Offers several videos in Spanish in the areas of Spanish and Latin American literature, history, and social studies. Keyword searches on the Web site using "Spanish" and "*Español*" bring up several hits.

Firefly Books Ltd. - P

3680 Victoria Ave.
Willowdale, Ontario, Canada
M2H 3K1
1-800-387-5085

Representing Bungalo Books, Annick Press, and Firefly Books, the Firefly Books catalog has several Spanish-language titles for board books, and children around five years of age.

Fisher Books - P

4239 W. Ina Rd. Suite 101
Tucson, AZ 85741; 1-800-255-1514
http://www.fisherbooks.com

Although the Spanish-language titles of this publisher are limited, they do include some apt topics: pregnancy and childbirth, prostate cancer, and *Life After Loss*.

Flame Co. - D

31 Marble Ave.
Pleasantville, NY 10570
1-800-535-2632
http://www.FlameCompany.com

Has a number of theme kits in English and Spanish, plus multi-ethnic dolls and stuffed animals to accompany books in both languages. The company also advertises its Super-FLAMEous Parents' Library-Spanish, with titles for adults needing parenting information for children of all ages. The way the system is set up, however, it might be more appropriate for clubs or organizations without a regular library staffed by a professional librarian.

Floricanto Press - P

650 Castro St., Suite 120-331
Mountain View, CA 94041-2055
415-552-1879
http://www.floricantopress.com

Besides *Bilindex*, the listing of Spanish-subject headings, Floricanto Press offers publications in the areas of history, literature, poetry, Cinco de Mayo, and reference. The Web site has improved since a first look at it.

Follett Library Book Company - D

4506 Northwest Highway
Crystal Lake, IL 60014-7393
1-800-435-6170
http://www.flr.follett.com

Carries Spanish-language titles for preschool through adult. Publishers and dates are indicated in the catalog, as are references to citations in standard review sources. Cataloging options are available.

Fondo de Cultura Económica USA, Inc. - P

2293 Verus St.
San Diego, CA 92154
1-800-5-FCEUSA
http://www.fceusa.com

Fondo de Cultura Económica is one of Mexico's government-run publishing houses. The children's catalog includes literature, translated into Spanish from a number of countries around the world, for preschoolers through high school, as well as a few Mexican textbooks for high school students. The adult catalog has listings for Mexican, Spanish, and Latin American literature, as well as a number of nonfiction topics.

Getty Education Institute for the Arts - P

1200 Getty Center Dr. Suite 600
Los Angeles, CA 90049-1683
1-800-223-3431
http://www.getty.edu/publications

The Multicultural Art Print Series offers five 18-by-24-inch posters on each of six topics. The Mexican-American and Women Artists of the Americas sets offer images of special relevance to Latinos.

Global Video, Inc. - D

P.O. Box FLL-4455
Scottsdale, AZ 85261
1-800-548-7123

Global Video has a selection of videos for youngsters just learning Spanish, popular movies dubbed into Spanish, and culturally relevant movies in English and Spanish that can serve as enrichment or to teach about events in the history of Latin American countries. For English-language learners, they offer several popular movies with spoken English and subtitles in Spanish.

Grolier Educational - P

90 Sherman Turnpike
Danbury, CT 06816
1-800-243-7256
http://publishing.grolier.com

Grolier offers the 14-volume set of *Nueva Enciclopedia Cumbre*, a Spanish-language encyclopedia with a Latin American viewpoint. Also: *Salvat Cuatro Diccionario Enciclopédico* and for younger students, the 10-volume *Everest Enciclopedia Escolar*. Cataloging services available.

Groundwood Books

Publishers Group West, 1700 Fourth St.
Berkeley, CA 94710
1-800-788-3123

Groundwood Books' imprint, *Libros Tigrillo*, promises to highlight children's books, either written or translated into Spanish, which relate to the lives of Spanish-speakers in the Americas.

Grupo Editorial Norma, P.R. - P

P.O. Box 195040
San Juan, PR 00919-5040

Norma's catalog describes series of books for preschoolers through young adults, many curriculum related. Also covered are CD-ROM programs including *Domine Diccionario Enciclopédico Interactivo* for ages seven and up and parenting materials.

Hampton-Brown - P

P.O. Box 369
Marina, CA 93933
1-800-333-3510
http://www.hampton-brown.com

"Hampton-Brown publishes titles in English and Spanish that are appropriate for early intervention reading programs" (Hampton-Brown catalog). Although geared for the classroom setting, the sets of materials for students in ESL, English literacy, and Spanish-literacy classes could be collected by any library serving children with those needs. Other materials include: Theme Packs, audiocassettes of songs and poems, poetry charts, and take-home parent packs.

Harper Libros - P

1000 Keystone Industrial Park
Scranton, PA 18512-4621
1-800-242-7737

Offers a number of fiction and nonfiction titles in Spanish for adults and children, including works by favorite authors Isabel Allende, Pat Mora, and Barbara Kingsolver.

High Haven Music - P

P.O. Box 246
Sonoita, AZ 85637-0246
520-455-5769

A selection of songs and stories on audiocassettes and in book form, most for younger students, but some also suitable for adults.

Ideal Foreign Books, Inc. - D

132-10 Hillside Ave.
Richmond Hill, NY 11418
718-297-7477

Has a small listing of materials for elementary students just beginning to read in Spanish, but the majority of titles deal with Spanish and Latin American literature and literary criticism.

Ingram Library Services, Inc. - D

P.O. Box 3006
One Ingram Blvd.
LaVergne, TN 37086-1986
1-800-937-5300

Ingram's *Libros en Español* magazine is published annually and provides an annotated listing of adult's and children's titles, grouped by subject category. The customer service representative can also provide such listings as only children's titles, titles by subject category, and Ingram's top 200 Spanish titles. Some of the popular automotive repair manuals are carried.

Innovative Choices Ltd., Inc. - D

6326 Sovereign Dr., Suite 138
San Antonio, TX 78229
1-800-519-2879
http://www.bookswithoutborders.com

The Internet bookstore features books, videos, and cassettes for children in Spanish, French, German, Italian, Russian, and English. No ISBNs are listed.

Inter-American Musical Editions

Cultural Office, Organization of American States
1889 F Street, NW
Washington, D. C. 20006

OAS has three CD sets of Latin American music in its Inter-American Music Editions.

Knowledge Unlimited, Inc.

P.O. Box 52
Madison, WI 53701-0052
1-800-356-2303

Although not geared toward LEP students, Knowledge Unlimited offers a selection of videos, posters, books, and multimedia kits to help students appreciate the cultural diversity of the United States.

L.E.A. Book Distributors - D

170-23 83rd Ave.
Jamaica Hills, NY 11432
718-291-9891
http://leabooks.com

A distributor of "major reference works for Hispanic studies;" the literature says they can secure any book published in Spain, Mexico, and Argentina. LEA carries several Spanish-language CD-ROM encyclopedias for children and adults, as well as other multimedia CD-ROM products, and, of course, books. The minimum order accepted from institutions is $200.

Larousse Kingfisher Chambers, Inc.
95 Madison Ave. Suite 1205
New York, NY 10016
1-800-497-1657

Kingfisher has a few Spanish-language titles for preschoolers and younger students.

Latin American Book Source, Inc. - D
48 Las Flores Drive
Chula Vista, CA 91910
619-426-1226

Most of the titles distributed by this source are frequently used in high school and college classes. Also distributes *Artes de México*, a quality serial publication from Mexico whose issues may be purchased on an individual basis or as a subscription.

Lectorum Publications, Inc. - P D
111 Eighth Ave. Suite 804
New York, NY 10011
1-800-345-5946
http://www.lectorum.com

Lectorum has an extensive collection of fiction and nonfiction for children and adults. It is also the exclusive distributor in the United States for cookbooks from Everest. Catalog card kits or MARC records with bar codes, as well as book processing are available.

Lee & Low Books - P
95 Madison Ave.
New York, NY 10016
212-779-4400
http://www.leeandlow.com

Specializing in multicultural literature for children, Lee & Low has titles in Spanish as well as English.

Library Video Co. - D
P.O. Box 580
Wynnewood, PA 19096
1-800-843-3620
http://www.libraryvideo.com

A selection of fiction and nonfiction videos suitable for preschool and up, including the *Tell Me Why Video Encyclopedia* series. Some titles have been dubbed in Spanish, whereas others have subtitles. MARC records and catalog card kits are available.

Librería & Distribuidora Universal - P D
3090 SW 8 St.
Miami, FL 33235
305-642-3234
http://www.ediciones.com

Publisher and distributor of Spanish-language materials for adults, with an emphasis on those with Cuban authors and themes. Also distributes material from *Fondo de Cultura Económica USA*, which offers a series of pocketbook titles for under $3.00 each in the latest catalog.

Libros Latinos - D
P.O. Box 1103
Redlands, CA 92373
1-800-MI-LIBRO

A source of used books on Latin American topics, most suitable for research needs.

Libros Sin Fronteras - D
P.O. Box 2085
Olympia, WA 98507-2085
360-357-4332
http://www.librossinfronteras.com

With an extensive collection of adult and children's books, spoken and music cassettes, and CDs categorized by subject, *Libros Sin Fronteras* offers an approval plan and core and opening-day collections. Brief citations in the catalog for each title include country and year of publication. For an additional charge, bindings can be reinforced. MARC records and cataloging are also available.

Live Oak Media
P.O. Box 652
Pine Plains, NY 12567
518-398-1010

Specializing in "quality media adaptations of outstanding . . . books" for children from kindergarten to fourth grade, Live Oak Media offers book/cassette read-along sets in English and Spanish. Cataloging is available for school library systems.

Llewellyn Español - P

P.O. Box 64383
St. Paul, MN 55164-0383
1-800-843-6666
http://www.llewellyn.com

Self-proclaimed as the "largest New Age Spanish-language publisher in the U.S."

Macmillan Children's Reference - P

Silver Burdett Press
P.O. Box 2649
Columbus, OH 43216-4843
1-800-848-9500

Offers a few Spanish-language titles for preschoolers on concepts such as colors, textures, numbers, and shapes.

Mariuccia Iaconi Book Imports, Inc. - D

970 Tennessee St.
San Francisco, CA 94107
1-800-955-9577
http://www.mibibook.com

Listed materials include everything for children from board books for preschoolers to fiction and texts for young adults. A-V materials include read-along sets, videos for young children, CD-ROMs from Dorling Kindersley, *Enciclopedia Interactive Santillana* CD-ROM, and *Aula Enciclopedia* CD-ROM (both encyclopedias for fourth grade and up). Rebinding and cataloging available as are sets of classroom libraries.

MEP Library Division - D

Midwest European Publications, Inc.
8220 N. Christiana Ave.
Skokie, IL 60076-2911
708-676-1199

MEP offers children's and adult literature in Spanish, French, German, Portuguese, and Italian. Spanish-language selections include favorite fairy tales translated from a number of other languages, book/tape selections, and novels for older students and adults by such authors as Michener, Stephen King, and Agatha Christie and well-known Latin Americans as Isabel Allende and García Márquez. Additional selections include materials for learning the just-listed languages, and reference materials.

Miller Educational Materials, Inc. - D

P.O. Box 2428
Buena Park, CA 90621
1-800-706-7568

The majority of the materials in this catalog are aimed at students and adults just learning English, but there are also Spanish and bilingual books, cassettes, and games that would complement a school's curriculum.

Multi-Cultural Books and Videos, Inc. - D

28880 Southfield Rd. Suite 183
Lathrup Village, MI 48076
1-800-567-2220
http://www.multiculbv.com

With materials in over 20 languages, including Spanish, this distributor offers Spanish-language and bilingual books, videos, audiocassettes, games, posters, and stickers for adults and children. Libraries serving high school and college students might be interested in the Shakespeare collection in which the videos of some of the more famous plays have been dubbed into Spanish. Also carries materials for learners of English.

NTC/Contemporary Publishing Group

4255 West Touhy Ave.
Lincolnwood, IL 60646-1975
1-800-323-4900
http://www.ntc-cb.com

Has selections of children's and adult books for foreign language study, ESL, GED, and basic reading.

Nana's Book Warehouse, Inc. - D

848 Heber Ave.
Calexico, CA 92231
1-800-737-NANA
http://www.quix.net/nanas/index.htm

Offering English, Spanish, and bilingual books for children through adults, with the emphasis on children; the bilingual annotations in Nana's catalog are fun to read. The catalog also offers other information such as book award winners and Mexican holidays.

National Educational Systems, Inc. - D
1711 Grandstand Dr.
San Antonio, TX 78238
1-800-442-2604

Provides books and other materials for English- and Spanish-literacy for children. Collections of books are available for younger students, but the catalog listings are mainly by title only.

NEWIST (Northeast Wisconsin In-School Telecommunications)
IS 1040, University of Wisconsin
Green Bay, WI 54311
1-800-633-7445
http://gbms01.uwgb.edu/~newist/index.html

Offers two Spanish-language children's videos on divorce and sexual abuse, for purchase or rental. Rather than relying on this Web site, a more reliable list of titles can be obtained by asking to be placed on their mailing list.

Nichols Publishing - P
1020 Andrew Dr. Suite 200
West Chester, PA 19380
1-800-695-1214
Fax: 610-738-9370

Publisher of *Chilton's Automotive* manuals in Spanish.

North-South Books - P
Distributed by: Chronicle Books
85 Second St.
San Francisco, CA 94105
1-800-722-6657
http://www.northsouth.com

Has some Spanish-language titles suitable for youngsters of preschool or early elementary ages.

Oxford University Press - P
ESL Department
200 Madison Ave.
New York, NY 10016
1-800-451-7556

Offers a variety of materials for children and adults just learning English.

PICS/The Project for International Communication Studies - D
The University of Iowa
270 International Center
Iowa City, Iowa 52242-1802
http://www.uiowa.edu/~pics

PICS has a selection of Spanish-language videotapes and video discs.

Planeta Publishing Corp.
939 Crandon Blvd.
Kay Biscayne, FL 33149
305-361-0053

Planeta offers some bilingual video series including *Inside Mexico* that includes eight titles dealing with various aspects of Mexican culture, and a children's video encyclopedia.

Pleasant Company Publications - P
P.O. Box 620991
Middleton, WI 53562-0991
1-800-257-3865 or 1-800-350-6555

The Josefina Books, part of the American Girls Collection, are available in English and Spanish and will help students gain an awareness of Southwest history and the role Hispanics have played in that history.

Quality Books Inc. - D
1003 W. Pines Rd.
Oregon, IL 61061-9680
1-800-323-4241

Can provide a list of children's and adult Spanish-language books. Each listing has a brief annotation, with the Spanish title also given in English.

Richard C. Owen Publishers, Inc. - P
P.O. Box 585
Katonah, NY 10536
1-800-336-5588
http://www.RCOwen.com

Geared toward an early elementary classroom with Spanish-speaking students, the books are available singly or in packets of 6 or 13 copies of each title.

Rodale Press - P
33 E. Minor St.
Emmaus, PA 18098
1-800-321-9299
http://www.rodalestore.com/bookstore/index.icl

Searching under the keyword "Spanish" on the Web site, one can find several health-related titles in Spanish.

Rourke Publishing Group - P
P.O. Box 3328
Vero Beach, FL 32964
1-800-394-7055
http://www.rourkepublishing.com

Rourke has a number of sets of Spanish-language, nonfiction books suitable for up to fifth grade. Books come with library binding, and cataloging is available.

Rusca Books – D
12315 Alston Dr.
Stafford, TX 77477
281-498-3156

Rusca carries books (including textbooks for pre-kindergarten through twelfth grade), A-V materials and computer software from a number of well-known Spanish language publishing houses. Most books come with library binding or it can be supplied for an additional fee.

Santillana USA Publishing Company, Inc. - P
2105 N.W. 86th Ave.
Miami, FL 33122
1-800-245-8584

Santillana, another major publisher from Spain, has a wide range of Spanish and bilingual books for students through high school. Included in their catalog are a number of Dorling Kindersley's Eyewitness Series (*Biblioteca Visual Altea*), *Enciclopedia Interactiva Santillana* on CD-ROM, and the *Richmond Electronic Dictionary: Spanish-English Bilingual Electronic Dictionary*, also on CD-ROM. These materials are also available from several of the distributors listed here.

Schoenhof's Foreign Books - D

76A Mount Auburn St.
Cambridge, MA 02138
617-547-8855
http://schoenhofs.com

Books for well-educated native speakers, or for serious students of foreign languages.

Scholastic, Inc.

555 Broadway
New York, NY 10012-3999
1-800-325-6149
http://www.scholastic.com

Publishers of a number of children's books in Spanish as well as sponsors of Book Fairs and Reading Clubs.

Shortland Publications, Inc. - P

50 S. Steele St. Suite 755
Denver, CO 80209-9927
1-800-775-9995
http://www.shortland.com

The *Storyteller* series, available in English and Spanish, "is a reading, writing, and language resource that enhances literacy learning" in primary grades.

Simon & Schuster - P

1230 Avenue of the Americas
New York, NY 10020
1-800-223-2348
http://simonandschuster.com

Offers a number of fiction and nonfiction titles for adults.

Smithsonian Folkways Recordings – P

Center for Folklife Programs and Cultural Studies
955 L'Enfant Plaza, Suite 73001
Washington, D.C. 20560-0953
202-287-2181
http://www.si.edu/folkways

The Smithsonian's collection of world folk traditions includes music from the Caribbean and Central and South America. Several of the recordings for children are done in a bilingual format.

Soleil Software, Inc.
3853 Grove Ct.
Palo Alto, CA 94303
1-800-501-0110
http://www.soleil.com

Soleil World Learning has four trilingual (Spanish, French, English) CD-ROM titles for ages 2 through 16 dealing, in fun settings such as a rainforest, Alaska, or safari, with different areas of the school curriculum.

Spanish Book Distributor, Inc.
8200 Southwestern Blvd. #1316
Dallas, TX 75206-2180
1-800-609-2180
http://www.sbdbooks.com

Although this distributor has books for both adults and children, the main emphasis appears to be on adult books in fields including fiction, practical issues, technical, reference, current issues, home and child care. SBD does carry at least one multimedia CD-ROM encyclopedia.

T. R. Books
822 N. Walnut Ave.
New Braunfels, TX 78130
1-800-659-4710

Distributes Spanish-language, interactive CD-ROMs from Dorling Kindersley, BBC Multimedia, Discovery Channel, and Zeta MultiMedia for preschoolers and up.

Tilbury House, Publishers
132 Water St.
Gardiner, ME 04345
1-800-582-1899
http://www.tilburyhouse.com

Offers a few parallel English and Spanish titles dealing with cultural diversity especially for elementary school students. Does offer volume discounts.

Time-Life
5240 W. 76th
Indianapolis, IN 43268-4137
1-800-277-8844
http://www.timelifeedu.com

Several of the *Time-Life* titles, suitable for kindergarten through 12th grade are available in Spanish, and could supplement your collection, especially if you already have the titles in English.

Tres Américas Books - D
4336 N. Pulaski Rd.
Chicago, IL 60641
773-481-9090

Trés Americas carries Spanish-language materials from Fondo de Cultural Económica USA as well as from Grupo Editorial Norma (see earlier descriptions).

TRI-LIN Integrated Services
6210 Stable Point Dr.
San Antonio, TX 78249
1-800-421-7842

Offers an extensive collection of A-V materials for Spanish-speakers including: charts for math, science, social studies, computers, reading, values development; decorations; and blank certificates. Also carries computer software suitable for preschooler through adult. The older student/adult software includes CD-ROMs for *Atlas Mundial Multimedia Salvat* and *Enciclopedia Multimedia Salvat,* as well as tutorials on using the Internet, Windows® 95, Word® and Excel®.

Unique Books Inc. - D
5010 Kemper Ave.
St. Louis, MO 63139
1-800-533-5446

Specializing in titles from small presses, Unique Books does offer some adult and children's titles in Spanish.

University of Wisconsin Hospital and Clinics – P
Dept. Of Outreach Education
702 N. Blackhawk Ave., Suite 215
Madison, WI 53705-3357
1-800-757-4354;
http://www.uwhealth.wisc.edu/outreach

    Offers a number of moderately priced videotape titles on various aspects of health, including two Spanish-language programs on cancer pain.

Vientos Tropicales & México Norte - D
P.O. Box 16176
Chapel Hill, NC 27516-6176
919-361-0997
http://www.vientos.com

    Specializes in supplying books from 19 northern Mexican states and seven Central American countries, with an emphasis on academic and primary-source materials. In some cases other resources such as serials, music CDs and CD-ROMs are also available. Materials are categorized only by subject groupings, and orders cannot yet be placed online.

■ Related Web Sites

Although it may not be feasible to order from these online sites, consulting them might be handy to help determine the availability of materials on specific subjects.

    Grupo Anaya (Spain): http://www3.anaya.es

        ISBN numbers are listed.

    Casa del Libro: http://www.casadellibro.com

        Another online bookstore, this one based in Madrid.

    Clearinghouse for Multicultural/Bilingual Education: http://www.weber.edu/MBE/Htmls/MBE-Books-Inter-Hispanic.html

        Links to agencies and companies offering information on books relating to Hispanic culture, although some of the links are out-of-date.

Editorial EDAF (Spain): http://arrakis.es/~edaf

ISBNs are listed for this publisher.

Espiral: www.espiral.com

An online bookstore serving both children and adults in Argentina, Columbia, Mexico, Venezuela, and the United States. Among the young adult titles listed were books by J. K. Rowling and J. R. Tolkien.

Fondo de Cultura Económica: http://www.fce.com.mx

No ISBN numbers are listed in the Web site, which is available in English and Spanish.

Librerías Gandhi: http://www.gandhi.com.mx

Search by title and author, however, no ISBN numbers are listed for this well-known Mexican bookstore chain.

Grijalbo: http://www.grijalbo.com.mx

Has titles in the following areas: practice books, myths, practical books, children's, novels, dictionaries, encyclopedia, and bestsellers. ISBNs listed.

InterLibros: http://www.interlibros.com.mx

Includes listing of bestsellers.

Jovellanos: http://www.j-libros.com

"The largest virtual bookstore in Mexico." Search the database by subject, author, or title.

Leer: http://www.leer.nisc.com

Leer is a free online search service published by National Information Services Corporation, Puerto Rico. Leer does not sell books, but does provide information as to where they are available.

Océano: http://www.oceano.com

ISBNs not listed. Has titles in areas of: art, history, and literature; CD-ROM; science; language study; reference materials; home; medicine and nursing; works for children and students; veterinary medicine and agriculture.

Grupo Patria Cultural: http://www.patriacultural.com.mx

ISBNs are given for listed titles.

Editorial Porrúa: http://www.porrua.com

Children's and adult titles are listed in this site from Mexico. ISBNs are given for all titles; bestsellers are listed under the heading *Novedades*.

Libreros Reunidos: http://www.barataria.com

This Web site from Spain advertises that it has nearly half a million titles from 720 publishers, but the only subjects one can access are bestsellers, children's books, medicine, women's books, and publications from the University of Alcalá. No summaries are given, just listings of titles.

Tematika: http://www.yenny.com.ar:80

A Mexican online bookstore with both adult and children's materials. Listed at the end of nearly every subject category are the Top Ten sellers of the week.

Virtual Family Website: http://www.familiavirtual.com.mxCComercial/ librerias.html

A Mexican Web site with links to approximately ten bookstores.

Yahoo's!® Spanish Language Booksellers http://dir.yhoo.com/Business_ and_Economy/Companies/Books/Shopping_and_Services/ Booksellers/ Languages/spanish

Web links to approximately 10 U.S. distributors of Spanish-language materials.

Bibliography

Abramoff, Carolann and Loraine Cors. Personal interview with author, Tampa Bay, Fla., 13 March 1999.

Acuña, Rodolfo. *Occupied America: A History of Chicanos*. New York: HarperCollins, 1988.

Ada, Alma Flor. *A Magical Encounter: Spanish-Language Children's Literature in the Classroom*. Compton, Calif.: Santillana, 1990.

Ada, Alma Flor. Personal interview, Denver, Colo., 24 April 1998.

Adam, Michelle. "Defining Latinidad: Collapsing the Walls of Latinismo," *Hispanic Outlook* (14 Aug. 1998): 7–9.

Adelante: Recommendations for Effective Library Service to the Spanish-Speaking. The California State Library Task Force on Serving Spanish-Speaking Communities, 1994.

Adelo, A. Samuel. "Emphasis on the Accent," *La Herencia del Norte* (Fall 1998): 54.

Agosto, Denise. "Bilingual Picture Books: Libros Para Todos," *School Library Journal* (Aug. 1997): 38–39.

Alire, Camila and Orlando Archibeque. *Serving Latino Communities: A How-To-Do-It Manual for Librarians*. New York: Neal-Schuman, 1998.

Allen, Adela Artola, editor. *Library Services for Hispanic Children: A Guide for Public and School Librarians*. Phoenix: Oryx Press, 1987.

———. "The School Library Media Center and the Promotion of Literature for Hispanic Children," *Library Trends* (Winter 1993): 437–455.

Alamonte, E. Ernest. Personal communication, 30 June 1998.

Alston, Gwendolyn and Herbert R. Lottman. "Spain's Small Miracles," *BookWire*. Aug. 15, 1998. [Online]. Available at: http://www.bookwire.com/pw/country-reports.article$25368 (Accessed Nov. 20, 1998).

Althaus, Dudley. "Twilight's Children: Debate Still Raging on Bilingual Education," *Houston Chronicle*. Dec. 14, 1995. [Online]. Available: http://www.chron.com/content/interactive/special/twilight/stories/part10.html (Accessed May 16, 1998).

Andrade de Herrara, Victoria. Education in Mexico: Historical and Contemporary Educational Systems. In *Children of La Frontera: Binational Efforts to Serve Mexican Migrant and Immigrant Students*. 1996. ERIC. (ED 393634)

131

Anhold, Susan. *Selecting Hispanic Books for School Libraries* (n.d.) Online]. Available: http://falcon.jmu.edu/~ramseyil/mulhispsel.htm (Accessed: Aug. 12, 1998).

Anstrom, Kris. *Preparing Secondary Education Teachers to Work with English Language Learners: Science.* Washington, D.C.: George Washington University, 1998.

Anzaldúa, Gloria. How to Tame a Wild Tongue. In *Out There: Marginalization and Contemporary Cultures,* by Russell Ferguson, et al. New York: New Museum of Contemporary Art, 1990.

Ashworth, Mary and H. Patricia Wakefield. *Teaching the World's Children: ESL for Ages Three to Seven.* Markham, Ontario: Pippin, 1994.

Aude, Laurie. Personal communication, 12 June 1998.

Barlow, Cara. " Ooooh Baby, What a Brain!" *School Library Journal,* 43:7 (1997): 20–22.

Barrera, Rosalinda B. "Profile: Pat Mora, Fiction/Nonfiction Writer and Poet," *Language Arts* (March 1998): 221–227.

Beilke, Patricia F. and Frank J. Sciara. *Selecting Materials For and About Hispanic and East Asian Children and Young People.* Hamden, Conn.: Library Professional Publications, 1986.

Benjamin, Rebecca. "Si Hablas Español Eres Mojado: Spanish as an Identity Marker in the Lives of Mexicano Children," *Social Justice* (Summer 1997): 26+.

Bermúdez, Andrea B. *Doing Our Homework: How Schools can Engage Hispanic Communities.* Charlestown, W. Va: ERIC Clearinghouse on Rural Education and Small Schools, 1994.

Bilindex: A Bilingual Spanish-English Subject Heading List. Oakland, Calif.: California Spanish Language Data Base, 1984.

Black, Susan. "Bilingual Education: Melting Pot or Salad Bowl?" *Education Digest* (March 1995): 53–56.

Blevins, Winfred. *Dictionary of the American West.* New York: Facts on File, 1993.

"The Book Scene in Mexico," *BookWire.* Sept. 1, 1998. [Online] Available: http://www.bookwire.com/pw/country-reports.article$25624 (Accessed: Nov. 20 1998).

Brown, Justine K. "Indigenous Connections through I*EARN," *Converge* (April 1999): 40–42.

Burgess, Larry. Telephone interview, 6 Oct. 1998.

Carrasquillo, Angela L. *Hispanic Children and Youth in the United States: A Resource Guide.* New York: Garland, 1991.

Cassady, Judith K. "Wordless Books: No-Risk Tools for Inclusive Middle-Grade Classrooms," *Journal of Adolescent & Adult Literacy* (March 1998): 428–432.

Chao, Sheau-yueh J. "The New Americans Program: Queens Borough Public Library's Service to Multilingual/Multicultural Communities," *Public Libraries* (Nov.-Dec. 1993): 319–322.

The Chicago Manual of Style. 14th edition. Chicago, University of Chicago Press, 1993.

Chickering, Sharon K. "One Tough Road," *Colorado Central* (Feb. 1997): 14–19.

Comi, Jennifer. Telephone interview, 14 Oct. 1998.

Constantino, Rebecca. "Two Small Girls, One Big Disparity," *The Reading Teacher* 48 (March 1995): 504–505.

———. "Learning to Read in a Second Language Doesn't Have to Hurt: The Effect of Pleasure Reading," *Journal of Adolescent & Adult Literacy* (Sept. 1995): 68–69.

———. " It's Like a Lot of Things in America': Linguistic Minority Parents' Use of Libraries," *School Library Media Quarterly* (Winter 1994): 87–89.

———. "A Study Concerning Instruction of ESL Students Comparing All-English Classroom Teacher Knowledge and English as a Second Language Teacher Knowledge," *The Journal of Educational Issues of Language Minority Students* (Spring 1994): 37–57.

———, editor. *Literacy, Access, and Libraries among the Language Minority Population.* Lanham, Md.: Scarecrow Press, 1998.

Cornejo, Ricardo J. "Bilingual Education: Some Reflections on Proposition 227," *Hispanic Outlook* (10 Oct. 1998): 27–32.

Council on Interracial Books for Children. *10 Quick Ways to Analyze Children's Books for Racism and Sexism.* n.d. [Online]. Available: http://www.birchlane.davis.ca.us/library/10quick.htm (Accessed May 14, 1998).

Cuello, José. *Latinos and Hispanics: A primer on terminology.* 1996. [Online]. Available: http://clnet.ucr.edu/library/reforma/refogold.htm#Why (Accessed Dec. 19, 1997).

Cumming, Peter. "Drop Everything and Read All Over: Literacy and Loving It," *The Horn Book Magazine* (Nov./Dec. 1997): 714–717.

Cummins, Jim. "Beyond Adversarial Discourse: Searching for Common Ground in the Education of Bilingual Students." Paper presented at Annual International Bilingual/Multicultural Education Conference of National Association for Bilingual Education, Denver, Colo., 28 Jan. 1999.

————. *Empowering Minority Students.* Sacramento, Calif.: California Association for Bilingual Education, 1989.

Dame, Melvina Azar. *The Role of the School Library in Serving LEP/ESL Students.* ERIC: 1994. ERIC. (ED 381033).

DeHerrera, Maria. Personal interview, Taos, N.M., 31 Oct. 1998.

"Día de los Niños: Día de los Libros," *REFORMA Newsletter* 17 (Summer 1998): 32.

Diez, Silvia and Aida Fernández. *Como Elevar la Capacidad de Aprendizaje del Estudiante a Través de las Artes del Lenguaje en Español.* Presentation given at Annual International Bilingual/Multicultural Education Conference, National Association of Bilingual Education, 29 Jan. 1999, Denver, Colo.

Directory of Resources on Library Services to the Spanish Speaking. Chicago: ALA, 1993.

Elder, Beth. Conversation with author, Denver, Colo., 4 May 1998.

Escobar Mamani, Maritza Elsa. Personal communication, Sept. 1998.

Everett, Peter. Personal communication, 11 May 1998.

"Facts on Hispanics," *The Voice of Hispanic Higher Education* (Feb. 1998): 8.

Fernández-Shaw, Carlos M. *The Hispanic Presence in North America from 1492 to Today.* New York: Facts on File, 1987.

Fox, Linda. "From Chants to Borders to Communion: Pat Mora's Poetic Journey to Nepantla," *Bilingual Review* 21, no. 3 (Sept., 1997): 219+.

Freiband, Susan J. "Developing Collections for the Spanish Speaking," *RQ* (Spring 1996): 330–342.

Gallegos, Bee and Lisa Kammerlocher. "A History of Library Services to the Mexican-American and Native American in Arizona," *Journal of the West* (July 1991): 79–89.

Gann, L. H. and Peter J. Duignan. *The Hispanics in the United States: A History.* Boulder, Colo.: Westview Press, 1986.

Gilbert, Deborah. "Migrant Workers Learn 'Survival English' from U-M Juniors and Seniors," *University of Michigan News & Info Services.* Sept. 1997. [Online]. Available: http://www.umich.edu/~news-info/U_Record/Issues97/Sep3_97/migrant.htm (Accessed: Jan. 26, 1999).

González, Christine. Telephone interview, 28 Sept. 1998.

González, Lucía. *Cultural Integration at the Library.* Presentation given at the Trejo Foster Foundation Hispanic Library Education Institute, 12 March 1999, Tampa, Fla. In: *Library Services to Youth of Hispanic*

Heritage, edited by Barbara Immroth and Kathleen de la Peña McCook. Jefferson, N.C.: McFarland, 2000.

Greenleaf, Janie et al. *Project MECHA: Distance Learning Linking Migrant Learning.* Presentation given at Annual International Bilingual/Multicultural Education Conference, National Association of Bilingual Education, 28 Jan. 1999, Denver, Colo.

Güereña, Salvador, editor. *Latino Librarianship: A Handbook for Professionals.* Jefferson, N.C.: McFarland, 1990.

Güereña, Salvador and Vivian Pisano. *Latino Periodicals.* Jefferson, N.C.: McFarland, 1998.

Guidelines for Selecting Bias-Free Textbooks and Storybooks. New York: Council on Interracial Books for Children, n.d.

Hamayan, Else V. and Ron Perlman. *Helping Language Minority Students After They Exit From Bilingual/ESL Programs: A Handbook for Teachers.* Washington, D. C.: National Clearinghouse for Bilingual Education, 1990.

Haro, Robert P. *Developing Library and Information Services for Americans of Hispanic Origin.* Metuchen, N.J.: Scarecrow Press, 1981.

Hayden, Carla D., editor. *Venture Into Cultures: A Resource Book of Multicultural Materials & Programs.* Chicago: ALA, 1992.

Headden, Susan. "The Hispanic Dropout Mystery: A Staggering 30 Percent Leave School, Far More Than Blacks or Whites. Why?" *U.S. News & World Report* (20 Oct. 1998): 64+.

Herrera, Julie and Margaret Morris. Request for Proposal: *Let's Collaborate? Challenge to Improve Learning Through Library Partnerships.* Alamosa Public Schools, Alamosa, Colo., 1997. Photocopy.

Hispanic Business (March 1998):16.

Holman, Linda J. "Meeting the Needs of Hispanic Immigrants," *Educational Leadership* (April 1997): 37+.

———. "Working Effectively with Hispanic Immigrant Families," *Phi Delta Kappan* (April 1997): 647+.

Holmes, Nora. Personal conversation with author, Colorado Springs, Colo., 29 Oct. 1998.

Hudelson, Sarah et al. "Chasing Windmills: Confronting the Obstacles to Literature-Based Programs in Spanish," *Language Arts* (March 1994): 164–171.

Igoa, Cristina. *The Inner World of the Immigrant Child.* New York: St. Martin's Press, 1995.

Jackson, Jack. *Los Mesteños: Spanish Ranching in Texas: 1721-1821.* College Station, Tex: Texas A & M University Press, 1986.

Johnston, James R. "Time to Ask! Library Service to Hispanic Patrons: A Beginning," *Illinois Libraries* (Fall 1993): 280–283.

Kiser, Karin N. "Country Reports: The USA Book Market in Spanish," *BookWire*, Oct. 15, 1998. [Online]. Available: http://www.bookwire.com/pw/country-reports.article$26126 (Accessed Nov. 20, 1998).

Krashen, Stephen. "Bilingual Education and the Dropout Argument." *Discover* (July 1998): 1–4.

Labodda, Marsha J. Personal communication, 17 June 1998.

Lance, Keith Curry, Lynda Wellborn and Christine Hamilton-Pennell. *The Impact of School Library Media Centers on Academic Achievement.* Denver: Colo. Dept. of Education, 1992.

Lanteigne, Betty and David Schwarzer. "The Progress of Rafael in English and Family Reading: A Case Study," *Journal of Adolescent & Adult Literacy* (Sept. 1997): 36–45.

Larson, Jeanette and Carolina G. Martinéz. "Hispanic_Kids@Library.net: Internet Resources for Latino Youth," *Youth Services in Libraries* (Spring 1998): 243–251.

Latin American Literature Pathfinder. Salt Lake City, Utah: Reforma de Utah, 1998.

Latin American Research and Service Agency. *LARASA/Report: A Publication About Latinos in Colorado* (Jan., Feb., July 1995; March, April, May 1997, June 1998).

Lodge, Sally. "Spanish-Language Publishing for Kids in the U.S. Picks Up Speed," *Publishers Weekly* 244 (25 Aug. 1997): S48+.

Lucas, Tamara. "What Have We Learned from Research on Successful Secondary Programs for LEP Students? A Synthesis of Finding from Three Studies," *Third National Research Symposium on Limited English Proficient Student Issues: Focus on Middle and High School Issues.* 1993 [online]. Available at: http://www.ncbe.gwu.edu/ncbepubs/symposia/third/lucas.htm (Accessed: Feb. 16, 1999).

Lynch, Mary Jo. "Using Public Libraries: What Makes a Difference?" *American Libraries* (Nov. 1997): 64, 66.

Martinez, Rosalie. Personal interview, Ft. Lupton, Colo., 18 May 1998.

McCain, Nancy. "Final Report: Hablanos Español: Outreach and Inclusion." Lake County Public Library, Leadville, Colo., 1996. Photocopy.

McCook, Kathleen de la Peña and Paula Geist. "Hispanic Library Services in South Florida," *Public Libraries* (Jan.-Feb. 1995): 34–37.

McQuillan, Jeff and Lucy Tse. "Child Language Brokering in Linguistic Minority Communities: Effects on Cultural Interaction, Cognition, and Literacy," *Language and Education*, 9 no.3 (1995); 195–215.

McWilliams, Carey. *North from Mexico: The Spanish-speaking people of the United States.* New York: Greenwood, 1990.

Mellander, Gustavo A. "Four Programs That Work: Keeping Students in School," *Hispanic Outlook* (5 June 1998): 4–5.

Mellander, Gustavo A. and Nelly Mellander. "Distance Learning Closing In," *Hispanic Outlook* (18 Dec. 1998): 9–11.

Mendosa, Rick. "What's Up With Teenagers?" *Hispanic Business* (July-Aug. 1998): 58–62.

Mestre, Lori S. and Sonia Nieto. "Puerto Rican Children's Literature and Culture in the Public Library," *MultiCultural Review* (June 1996): 26–39.

Miller, Berna. "Educating Immigrant Children: It's Got To Be Done," *Current* (Jan. 1998): 3–7.

Miller, Terry. "The Place of Picture Books in Middle-level Classrooms," *Journal of Adolescent & Adult Literacy* (Feb. 1998): 376–381.

Minicucci, Catherine and Laurie Olsen. *Programs for Secondary Limited English Proficient Students: A California Study.* Washington, D. C.: National Clearinghouse for Bilingual Education, 1992.

Miramontes, Ofelia B., Adel Nadeau, and Nancy L. Commins. *Restructuring Schools for Linguistic Diversity: Linking Decision Making to Effective Programs.* New York: Teachers College Press, 1997.

Moles, Oliver C., editor. *Reaching All Families: Creating Family-Friendly Schools.* Washington, D. C.: U.S. Dept of Education, 1996.

Mora, Pat. "Confessions of a Latina Author," *The New Advocate* (Fall 1998): 279–290.

———. Conversation with author, Steamboat Springs, Colo., 12 Sept. 1998.

———. "Día de los Niños: Día de los Libros: Bilingual Literacy Day," *United States Board on Books for Young People, Inc. Newsletter* (Spring 1998): 15–18.

Morales, Diana. Telephone interview, 26 March 1999.

Morgan, Dawn-Leigh. "Se Habla Español," Hobbs, N.M. *News-Sun,* 1 May 1994, 17.

Mulhern, Margaret, Flora V. Rodriguez-Brown, and Timothy Shanahan. "Family Literacy for Language Minority Families: Issues for Program Implementation," *NCBE Program Information Guide Series,* Number 17, Summer 1994.[Online]. Available: http://www.ncbe.gwu.edu/ncbepubs/pigs/pig17.htm (Accessed Dec. 12, 1998).

Murphy, Patrick D. "Conserving Natural and Cultural Diversity: The Prose and Poetry of Pat Mora," *MELUS* (Spring 1996): 59+.

Nathenson-Mejia, Sally. "Bridges Between Home and School: Literacy Building Activities for Non Native English Speaking Homes," *The Journal of Educational Issues of Language Minority Students* (Winter 1994): 149–164.

National Center for Education Statistics. *Digest of Education Statistics 1995.* Lanham, Md.: U.S. Dept. of Education, 1995.

National Center for Family Literacy. *When Families Learn Together.* (n.d.) [Online]. Available: http://ericps.ed.uiuc.edu/npin/respar/texts/parfami/famlearn.html (Accessed: Jan. 18, 1999).

National Education Association. *NEA: Read Across America - 1998 Highlights.* (n.d.) [Online]. Available: http://www.nea.org/readacross/ideas.html (Accessed Dec. 31, 1998).

Navarrette, Yolanda Gómez. "Family Involvement in a Bilingual School," *The Journal of Educational Issue of Language Minority Students* (Summer 1996). [Online]. Available: http://www.ncbe.gwu.edu/miscpubs/jeilms/vol16/jeilms1606.htm (Accessed Dec. 14, 1998).

No More Excuses: The Final Report of the Hispanic Dropout Project. [Washington, D.C.]: U.S. Dept. of Education, 1998.

Orellana, Marjorie Faulstich. "¡Aquí Vivimos!: Voices of Central American and Mexican Participants in a Family Literacy Project," *The Journal of Educational Issue of Language Minority Students* 17 (Summer 1996).

Ortiz, Margarita. Personal communication, 15 May 1998.

Osius, Lucy. Personal conversation, Leadville, Colo., 18 Sept. 1998.

Oslund, Janet. Telephone conversation, 24 March 1999.

Otero Guzmán, Milagros. Library Services to the Youth in Puerto Rican Public Libraries. Paper presented at the Trejo Foster Foundation Hispanic Library Education Institute in Tampa, FL, March 1999. In *Library Services to Youth of Hispanic Heritage*, edited by Barbara Immroth and Kathleen de la Peña McCook. Jefferson, N.C.: McFarland, 2000.

Our Nation on the Fault Line: Hispanic American Education, Sept. 1996. [Online]. Available: http://www.ed.gov/pubs/FaultLine/call.html (Accessed: April 2, 1998).

Parry Jean. Conversation with the author, Leadville, Colo., 16 March 1999.

Patterson, Irania Macías. "The Public Library of Charlotte and Mecklenburg County Speaks Español," *North Carolina Libraries, the Professional Journal of the North Carolina Library Association* 56 (Winter 1998): 145–147.

Payne-Button, Linda. Telephone interview, 13 Oct. 1998.

Peterson, Verla. Personal conversation with the author, Taos, N.M., 31 Oct. 1998.

Pombo, Rebecca Tellez. Personal communication, 14 May 1998.

Ponce, Mary Helen. "Latina Librarians," *Saludos Hispanos* (Sept.-Oct. 1998): 16–17+.

Pucci, Sandra L. "Supporting Spanish Language Literacy: Latino Children and Free Reading Resources in Schools," *Bilingual Research Journal* (Winter-Spring 1994): 67–82.

Ramirez, Melva and Frances Smardo Dowd. "Another Look at the Portrayal of Mexican-American Females in Realistic Picture Books: A Content Analysis, 1990-1997," *MultiCultural Review* (Dec. 1997): 20–27+.

Reforma: The National Association to Promote Library Services to the Spanish Speaking. 1996. [Online]. Available: http://clnet.ucr.edu/library/reforma/refogold.htm#Why (Accessed: Dec. 19, 1997).

Reforma de Utah. *Latin American Literature Pathfinder.* Westpointe, Utah: Reforma de Utah, 1998.

Rey, Clara. Personal conversation, Taos, N.M., 31 Oct. 1998.

Rigg, Pat and Virginia G. Allen, editors. *When They Don't All Speak English: Integrating the ESL Student into the Regular Classroom.* Urbana, Ill.: National Council of Teachers of English, 1989.

Rivera, Martín. Telephone interviews, 24 July 1998; 10 Nov. 1998.

Rodriguez, Jill and Maria Tejeda. "Serving Hispanics Through Family Literacy: One Family ata Time," *Illinois Libraries* (Fall 1993): 331–335.

Rodriguez, Judith. "Books for Young Adults: Libros Para Adolescentes," *REFORMA Newsletter* (Summer 1995): 7.

Romberg, Raquel. "Saints in the Barrio: Shifting, Hybrid, and Bicultural Practices in a Puerto Rican Community," *MultiCultural Review* (June 1996): 16–23.

Roslow, Peter and J. A. F. Nicholls. "Targeting the Hispanic Market: Comparative Persuasion of TV Commercials in Spanish and English," *Journal of Advertising Research* (May-June 1996): 67+.

Sanchez, Saadia et al. *Public Library Services for Latino Young Adults.* Berkeley: University of California School of Library and Information Studies, 1989.

Sayers, Dennis. "Language Choice and Global Learning Networks: The Pitfall of *Lingua Franca* Approaches to Classroom Telecomputing," *Education Policy Analysis Archives* 3 (10) 1995. [Online]. Available: http://olam.ed.asu.edu/epaa/v3n10.html (Accessed Dec. 31, 1998).

Scarborough, Katharine T. A.. *Developing Library Collections for California's Emerging Majority: A Manual of Resources for Ethnic Collection Development.* Berkely, Calif.: University of California, Berkeley School of Library and Information Studies, 1990.

Schon, Isabel. *The Best of the Latino Heritage: A Guide to the Best Juvenile Books about Latino People and Cultures.* Lanham, Md.: Scarecrow Press, 1997.

———. *Recommended Books in Spanish for Children and Young Adults, 1991-1995.* Lanham, Md.: Scarecrow Press, 1997.

———. *Books in Spanish for Children and Young Adults: An Annotated Guide. Series VI.* Metuchen, N.J.: Scarecrow Press, 1993.

———. *A Bicultural Heritage: Themes for the Exploration of Mexican and Mexican-American Culture in Books for Children and Adolescents.* Metuchen, N.J.: Scarecrow Press, 1978.

———. "Spanish-Language Books for Young Readers - Great Expectations, Disappointing Realities," *Booklist* (1 Oct. 1995): 318–319.

———, editor. *Contemporary Spanish-Speaking Writers and Illustrators for Children and Young Adults: A Biographical Dictionary.* Westport, Conn.: Greenwood, 1994.

Schwartz, Wendy. "Hispanic Preschool Education: An Important Overview," *ERIC Digest.* Urbana, Ill.: ERIC Clearinghouse on Urban Education, n.d.

Seda, Milagros and Dennis J. Bixler-Marquez. "The Ecology of a Chicano Student at Risk," *The Journal of Educational Issues of Language Minority Students* 13 (Spring 1994): 195–208.

Shapiro, Michael. "What About the Library Market?" *Publishers Weekly* (25 Aug. 1997): S47.

Shorris, Earl. *Latinos: A Biography of the People.* New York: W. W. Norton, 1992.

Silva-Díaz, María Cecilia. "Rites of Initiation in Recent Latin American Narratives," *Bookbird* (Summer 1997): 21–26.

Silvey, Anita, editor. *Children's Books and Their Creators.* New York: Houghton Mifflin, 1995.

Skutnabb-Kangas, Tove and Jim Cummins, editors. *Minority Education: From Shame to Struggle.* Clevedon, Avon, England: Multilingual Matters Ltd., 1988.

Somerville, Mary R. "Global is Local," *Library Journal* (15 Feb. 1995): 131–133.

Sosa, Alicia. *Thorough and Fair: Creating Routes to Success for Mexican-American Students.* Charleston, W.Va.: ERIC Clearinghouse on Rural Education and Small Schools, 1993.

Struthers, Sue. Telephone interview, 10 Nov. 1998.

Sundell, Jon. Personal conversation, Tampa, Fla., 13 March 1999.

Suro, Roberto. *Strangers Among Us: How Latino Immigration is Transforming America*. New York: Alfred Knopf, 1998.

Tabor, Nancy. *Enhancing Cultural Awareness Through Children's Books*. Presentation given at Annual International Bilingual/Multicultural Education Conference, National Association of Bilingual Education, 28 Jan. 1999, Denver, Colo.

Tauler, Sandra. Telephone interview, 22 Oct. 1998.

Taylor, Sally. "A Brave New World of Books," *Publishers Weekly* (25 Aug., 1997).

———. "In Search of the Spanish Market," *Publishers Weekly* (25 Aug., 1997).

Texas State Library. *Día de los Niños: Día de los Libros*. (n.d.) [Online]. Available: http://www.tsl.state.tx.us/LD/Publications/ninos/title.htm (Accessed April 10, 1998).

Tinajero, Josefina Villamil and Alma Flor Ada, editors. *The Power of Two Languages: Literacy and Biliteracy for Spanish-Speaking Students*. New York: Macmillan McGraw-Hill School Publishing, 1993.

Treviño, Rose. Telephone interview, 29 March 1999.

Tse, Lucy. "The Effects of Ethnic Identity Formation on Attitudes toward Ethnic Language Development." 1996. ERIC. (ED 394344).

———. "Language Brokering Among Latino Adolescents: Prevalence, Attitudes, and School Performance," *Hispanic Journal of Behavioral Sciences* 17 (2 May 1995): 180–193.

———. "When an ESL Adult Becomes a Reader," *Reading Horizons* 37 no. 1(1996): 16–29.

———. "When Students Translate for Parents: Effects of Language Brokering," *CABE Newsletter* 17 (Jan. - Feb. 1995): 16–17.

Tse, Lucy and Jeff McQuillan. "Culture, Language and Literacy: The Effects of Child Brokering on Language Minority Education." Paper presented at annual meeting of the American Educational Research Association, 8–12 April 1996, at New York, N.Y.

Tuleja, Tad. *Foreignisms: A Dictionary of Foreign Expressions Commonly (and Not So Commonly) Used in English*. New York: Stonesong Press, 1989.

U.S. Bureau of the Census. The Hispanic Population in the United States: Population Characteristics. Feb. 2000 [Online] Available: http://www.census.gov/prod/2000pubs/p20-527.pdf

U.S. Bureau of the Census. *Resident Population of the United States: Estimates, by Sex, Race, and Hispanic Origin, with Median Age*. 30 April 1998. [Online]. Available: http://www.census.gov/population/estimates/nation/intfile3-1.txt (Accessed May 16, 1998).

————. *Selected characteristics of all persons and Hispanic persons, by type of origin: March 1996.* Feb. 3, 1998. [Online]. Available: http://www.census.gov/population/socdemo/hispanic/cps96/sumtab-2.txt (Accessed: May 16, 1998).

————. *United States Dept. of Commerce News.* April 1997. [Online]. Available: http://www.census.gov/Press-Release/cb97-55.html (Accessed: May 16, 1998)

————.*Statistical Abstract of the United States.: 1997* (117th edition). Washington, D.C., 1997.

————. *Statistical Abstract of the United States: 1999* (119th edition.) Washington, D.C., 1990.

Uquillas, Guadalupe. Personal communication. 28 April 1998.

Wallace, Suby. "I've Had the Best Week." In LM_NET [Online listserv, accessed Oct. 20, 1998]; available from LM_NET@listserv.syr.edu.

White, Cherie R. Personal communication. 5 May 1998.

Williams, Norma. *The Mexican American Family: Tradition and Change.* Dix Hills, N.Y.: General Hall, Inc., 1990.

Zwick, Louise Yarian and Oralia Garza de Cortés. "Library Programs for Hispanic Children," *Texas Libraries* (Spring 1989): 12–16.

Index